Signature Golf Swing: Stop fighting with complicated swing mechanics!

Build your own golf swing by simplifying the basics to naturally hit longer and straighter, injury free.

by Lee Kopanski

Kopanski Publishing

Signature Golf Swing: Stop fighting with complicated swing mechanics!

Published by Kopanski Publishing

www.leekopanski.com
www.golfswingzone.com

Copyright © 2012 Lee Kopanski. All Rights Reserved.

No part of this publication may be reproduced, stored in a retrieval system or transmitted in any form or by any means, electronic, mechanical, photocopying, recording, scanning or otherwise. This book is sold subject to the condition that it shall not, by trade or otherwise, be lent, re-sold, hired out or otherwise circulated in any form of binding or cover other than that in which it is published and not without the express prior written permission of the publisher.

Disclaimer: Every effort has been made to accurately reflect the qualities and potential of this product and although such proven teaching methods significantly improve performance at all levels from beginner to professional, success cannot be guaranteed and is dependent upon many factors including (but not limited to) your health and general fitness, your level of skill and expertise, the time and commitment you dedicate to your progress and the extent to which you follow the guidelines in this improvement system as instructed. Any participation is at your own risk and no liability is assumed whatsoever for your actions. You should consult a doctor if you have any health concerns at any time prior to or during the implementation of this product.

ISBN: 978-0-9569633-3-8

<u>Also by Lee Kopanski:</u>

**3 Steps Correct Your Golf Swing:
Guaranteed to correct any swing fault in 3 simple steps.**
Banish your slice, hook, pull, pull hook, push, shank and topped, heavy and skyed shots forever.

**Short Game MASTER Class
PLUS A Golf Shot For Every Shot**
*30 shots to cover every situation.
You'll never be out of the game again!*

Available at www.leekopanski.com

For free premium online golf lessons visit www.golfswingzone.com

A Few Words...

"As several times Austrian middle-distance running Champion I have a renewed excitement and love for sport at the age of 52. A friend introduced me to the game of golf, and after taking some useful lessons, I began to buy books to immerse myself into the subject and improve my swing. My frustration mounted as I had to think about 10 things at the same time during my swing and my success was limited until I had the opportunity to meet a Pro by the name of Lee Kopanski. In two lessons he was able to show me how simple the golf swing can be. I was not only impressed by the simplicity of Lee's teaching methods, but also by his enthusiasm, dedication and love of golf. His book **(Signature Golf Swing)** is a masterpiece. In one season alone I dropped 20 shots and I know that thanks to his teaching system I will be a single figure handicapper by the end of this season. Thank you Lee, you are the best!"

Gerhard Holzknecht (Austria)

Marathon winner (2,000 participants) Riccione, Italy. Several times Austrian middle-distance running champion and trainer of Olympic, European and World Championship competitors. Gerhard has competed across London, Europe and USA and received invitations to study in the USA. He contributes to specialist magazines and has trained with Sebastian Coe, Steve Ovett, Steve Cram, Markus Ryffel, Mike Boit and other world-class athletes.

"I have played golf and took golf lessons for over twenty years so there's not much I haven't heard or tried. Lee's teaching methods on the other hand were a breath of fresh air I don't think about my hips, shoulders or any of the other complicated stuff. In just one season I dropped from Hcp 17 to Hcp 8 following his simple instruction using his guides and controls, I am made up, I owe you a few beers, cheers Lee!"

Joe Doyle (London)

"I injured my lower back years ago playing Rugby and I thought that was the reason it hurt so much after a round of golf. Found Lee's online lessons searching google only to find out that my golf swing was the cause of the pain. Made a few simple changes and no more pain and my whole game has improved ten fold. Lee where have you been could of done with you ten years ago, great stuff!"

Alan Rigby (Cardiff)

"All I wanted was a golf swing that works so that I don't make a total fool of myself in front of my two twenty year old lads. I was sceptical of online golf lessons but have to say I am enjoying my golf more than ever now that my Slice has gone. I caught my eldest son (Hcp 5) practicing with the guides and controls that says it all or maybe it was my first Birdie. Lee's **Signature Golf Swing** book is not just a book but rather a series of easy to follow golf lessons that I can't rave about enough and I don't rave easily! Thanks a million!"

Bill Glover (Nottingham)

"As a Scratch player for many years I have always found it hard to control the clubface throughout my backswing. I bought your **Signature Golf Swing** 3 months ago, got to say the lesson on wrists hinge was worth every penny, top class. I have had numerous golf lessons with some top class golf coaches (which don't come cheap) but after working through your teaching methods my ball striking and consistency off the tee is the best it's ever been, awesome!"

Jason Green (Sidney)

"**Signature Golf Swing** was recommended to me by a golf buddy actually it was my last hope. I played soccer, tennis and basketball all to a high standard but golf just killed me. Lee, I have watched DVD's, read books and searched the internet but nothing made sense. I studied sports science so I know what I'm talking about, your methods make complicated, simple! When can I get your lessons on DVD? You have turned a hacker into a 12 Hcp in one season! Rock on!"

Brendan Jackson (New York)

www.golfswingzone.com

Signature Golf Swing: Stop fighting with complicated swing mechanics!

"My Slice was killing my game and was losing me massive amounts of distance. I had 1 lesson with Lee and immediately started to hit longer and straighter than ever. My drives were accurate, the Slice had vanished and my new found length left my playing partners scratching their heads! Lee's teaching methods worked wonders for me and the highlight was being presented with the green jacket and crowned **Senior Austrian Masters champion 2010**."

Hans Tritscher, 2010 Masters Tournament Champion
ÖGS (Austrian Seniors Golf Association)

"Hello Lee, I have searched far and wide and tried many things before discovering your **Signature Golf Swing** teaching system. I followed it exactly, lesson for lesson, it is amazing how easy golf can be. At the beginning of the season a par 72 course took me 127 shots, but thanks to your book (I have never taken a personal lesson with you) at the end of the season I am regularly playing rounds of 90 shots. Brilliant!"

Ronald Pischof (Graz, Austria)

"It is essential that your basic golf techniques are correct, especially when you don't have the opportunity to play as regularly as you'd like. Lee knows exactly how to focus on the main elements of a shot and explains point for point what needs to be done. When my game is not going as well as I would like I remind myself of his words and find my way back into the game."

Jürgen Demuth (Vienna, Austria)

"**Signature Golf Swing** has allowed me to take a major step forward in my golf. I have focused on a few extremely important points and have noticed a marked improvement in my swing. At the end of the day I am happy with my score and much more importantly, my golf is great fun!"

Marion Dolezal (Vienna, Austria)

"I thought I was a "has been" having once played off a steady 2 Hcp then I totally lost it. My handicap crept up every year and it was that bad at one stage that I didn't touch a club for 8 months. I found Lee Kopanski on the web and thought he would be churning out the same old techniques that I was tired of hearing about. Got to give it to you Lee your lessons are top notch and for the most part new to me. The lesson on core rotation is simply fantastic and with the help of your **Signature Golf Swing** book I am back to striking the ball just like the good old days and I'm now chasing that 2 Hcp!"

Simon Evans (Kent, UK)

As a golf Profesional constantly striving to improve my unique teaching system
I welcome all of your ideas, suggestions and feedback which you can e-mail
directly to me at at pro@golfswingzone.com.

Your comments may well appear in a future edition!

For all the latest news and information visit www.leekopanski.com

 www.golfswingzone.com

Table of Contents

Who am I to teach you Golf?..iv

Inspiration vi

Swing Myth Demolition 1
Swing Myth 1: Swing on the line of your target 1
Swing Myth 2: Keep your head down and still 7
Swing Myth 3: Hitting down on the ball.................................10
Swing Myth 4: The straight left arm 12
Swing Myth 5: Low and slow 14
Swing Myth 6: Pull down with your left hand 16
Swing Myth 7: The Perfect swing 18

Dynamic Foundation 21
Clubface alignment: Don't just stab in the dark....................21
Grip pressure: Please don't release me or let me go!!.........26
The Golf grip for your hands 27
Posture: Alive and kicking 30
Ball position: Play the easy ball 37
Stance: Stand to deliver 39
Stand to attention..41

Signature Swing 43
Every golf swing is like a signature! 43
Your ball is not alive 44
Play the dead ball 45
Develop instinctive feeling for your target 46
The Target 47

Signature Swing: 1st Gear 49
Signature Swing: From the ground up...................................49
Signature Swing: Dynamic set up 51
Signature Swing: Mindset of greatness..................................52
Signature Swing: 1st Gear backswing 54
Signature Swing: 1st Gear downswing; Let down.................61
Signature Swing: 1st Gear downswing; Angle of attack.................66
Signature Swing: Downswing; Move through the gears 68
Signature Swing: 1st Gear: Downswing direction 70

Signature Swing: 2nd Gear 73
Signature Swing: 2nd Gear: Clubface alignment 73
True impact 78
Signature Swing: 1st and 2nd Gears; Step up to the challenge 79
Eyes wide shut! 82

Signature Swing: 3rd Gear 83
Swing Myth 8: The Tiger effect 83
The Mirror never lies 85
Signature Swng: 3rd Gear half swing; Body 87

Signature Swing: 4th Gear 93
Swing Myth 9: Perfectly still and 90 93
Signature Swing: Core rotation 94
Swing Myth 10: The Biggest cock-up 97
Signature Swing: The Power in transition 100
Drive to top gear 105
Signature Swing: 4th Gear; Personality 106
Signature Swing: 4th Gear; Up to full 108
True impact up to top gear 115

Signature Swing: 5th Gear 121
Signature Swing: 5th Gear; Power in transition 121
Pack on the muscle: Power in transition 124

Top Gear 127
Signature Swing: Master plan 128
The Zone 131
Your Golf Swing Zone: Key Elements 132
Time zone 140

Who am I to teach you Golf?

Alan Thompson, English National Elite Coach

"I have known Lee for seven years as a pupil and a Golf Professional. During this time I have seen him work diligently on his technique with an intensity and commitment given to very few people. This same quality is evident in his conduct around the Pro's Shop and in his own teaching where I know his attention to detail and enthusiasm for the job at hand ensures that his clients receive the very best of attention." (1998)

Alan Thompson has inspired many England International junior boys and several England girls and ladies, including two Curtis Cup players. He is coach to many European Tour Professionals, PGA Professionals and to the England National Elite A Squad. Much of the future of English golf rests in his hands.

I worked together with Alan Thompson, the English National Elite Coach, to both improve my own skills as a player and also to gain the knowledge required to develop my skills as a Professional Coach. I predominantly learned from Alan Thompson how vital it is to nurture a golfer's own stylistic individuality whist at the same time ensuring that their basic fundamentals are rock solid. I still find today that this is the best way to unlock true potential at every level of ability. We are all individual so therefore every golfer has to "find their own swing" which is a golf swing made to measure, to fit the personality, style and make-up of the player.

Denis Pugh, PGA *MASTER Professional

"Lee Kopanski regularly visited me for golf instruction over a 14 month period during the time I was based at the Warren Golf Club in Essex. Lee made a big effort to travel from his home in the North of England and thereby proved his commitment to improving both his golf swing and his knowledge of teaching. His understanding of the mechanics of the golf swing plus his interest in the skills of teaching will, I am sure, serve him well in the future." (2000).

Denis Pugh is the renowned golf analyst on Sky Sports Golf Night and was a former tour player himself. He has coached over 150 Tour Professionals since 1988. He is most famous for his long time association with 8 time European Order of Merit winner and Ryder Cup Captain Colin Montgomerie.

I worked together with Denis Pugh PGA MASTER Professional to further my knowledge of teaching and to improve my skills as a tournament Professional. From Denis Pugh I learned (in particular) about the game of golf in greater technical detail and about how to distinguish the key elements of an individual's golf swing which will ultimately make or break him. Denis Pugh taught me that swing analysis is vital to the improvement of golfers at all levels, and in the process of fine tuning a golf swing. However, many over-step the mark into the world of over-analysis which can be highly detrimental to a player's development. From this education I developed a keen eye for technical detail without crossing the fine line into over-analysis whilst at the same time ensuring that a player's instinct and natural ability remain at the forefront throughout.

Bill Ferguson, PGA *MASTER Professional

"I have known Lee Kopanski for the past two years and I have also taught him not only about his personal golf swing, but about the golf swing in general. I found him to be a very personable young man, articulate and well mannered." (2000).

There are not many people who can claim Colin Montgomerie as a caddy but Bill Ferguson can. Bill was Monty's first mentor as a nine-year old and coached him well into his professional career. Bill Ferguson's playing highlights include lifting the PGA Club Professional Championship in 1976. He was the English national coach for 25 years and is a past Yorkshire captain of the PGA as well as serving on the executive committee. Bill Ferguson has been a mentor to many great players including; Colin Montgomerie, Ian Woosnam, Howard Clark, Darren Clarke, Paul Broadhurst and the legendary Seve Ballesteros.

Signature Golf Swing: Stop fighting with complicated swing mechanics!

Working with Bill Ferguson PGA MASTER Professional provided me with yet another perspective into world class elite coaching, further developing both my professional playing ability and teaching career. Bill Ferguson is an exceptional coach and his track record speaks for itself. Many of the techniques that I learned from Bill Ferguson cannot be found in a text book but rather have been acquired over years of hands on experience working with some of the best players to have ever graced a fairway. It is impossible for me to sum up in a few words the extent of the knowledge that I gained from such a master coach. Bill Ferguson opened my eyes to a new world of just how simple the game of golf can be. I learned that ultimately the ball is the best teacher yet only when you learn to read its flight correctly can you then trace back to the golf swing that created it. Bill Ferguson is not purely a master of the swing but also a short game wizard who often goes against conventional wisdom. For the record, the legendary Seve Ballesteros was once his pupil. I think that says it all.

***MASTER** **Professional. Awarded by the PGA to qualified members held in high national or international esteem. Members that have made a significant contribution to the development of golf as a player, coach, administrator or course designer. A leader in their field for a number of years. An innovator.**

Inspiration

I wanted to speak to you, the passionate people who are really striving to make a difference by improving themselves.

My dream was to be the best, to conquer the world, to lift the claret jug high above my head. Golf waits for no man, unquestionable dedication and the will to win alone is often not enough to be your best. I learnt too late that success revolves around mastering what works for you the way that Mother Nature intended. Constantly locking yourself in a fight with swing mechanics jumping from one magic move to the next is a painful lesson, learned the hard way. The clock is constantly ticking; if you're not good enough fast enough in this world then the truth of the matter is; *time is money and money is time*. My passion was spun and thrown into another direction. I discovered that to nurture and support a dream is a dream come true, *life without a dream is a life never lived*!

As a highly driven individual I push my limits extremely hard to improve myself. As a result I have had the pleasure of learning my trade with some very talented individuals who are held in the highest regard in the world of golf. If I'm honest, you might be surprised to learn that this is not all about you. This is my personal quest to discover how I got lost and where I went wrong. I am here to prove a point and prevent the same thing from happening to another strong ambition with bright eyes and a firm hold on a distant dream.

Experience has taught me how easy it is to waste a lot of time and energy, amongst other things, on improving your golf. This game is a mine field and I am here to set the record straight, to challenge techniques thought to be key and fundamental by many. To play great golf you don't have to be the talent of the century or have the eye of the tiger but, as with anything in life, you shouldn't do anything until you know what you are doing. Hanging from the tree tops all night long will not make your arms significantly longer, you are who you are, don't fight it, you should never try to be someone you are not. Through intense practice I was (and still am) more than familiar with the ever new hot tips and tricks to line the book shelves, only to discover that the majority were a total scam for the so called "expert", who was just as confused as me, to hide behind.

As a kid I would stand up to the ball, have a quick look at my target and nail it, without a care in the world. It's only now that I understand what happened to the boy who played the game of golf from instinctive feeling; he got lost and totally disorientated, as many do in the world of over analysis, swing mechanics, angles and rotations. The game of golf was no longer a game but rather a mathematical equation that didn't seem to add up as I constantly tied myself up in knots that a black belt would be proud of. My talent and instinct were ripped from my grasp. I was so wrapped up in technical details that I began to question which end of the golf club I should grip. This is a lifeboat that I am sending out to you, better to save one man than to save none at all.

Before I go any further I am not going to apologise for my sometimes hard-hitting attitude. My wife (who is nearly always right) tells me that at times I sound too abrupt without firstly considering your feelings and without taking the feelings of others into consideration. I have always been hard on myself and believe that to improve yourself you have to have a combination of being hard and honest, to really get the best from yourself.

If you can't laugh at yourself or you are easily offended then my wife is really sorry. If you really want to improve I want you to open yourself up to some new ideas that will change the way you play golf forever. I don't see the point in beating about the bush. You are here to learn how to play golf the way your body was made to, not to be taken on a magical mystery tour. Please get ready for some home truths that I wish I was introduced to the first time I held a golf club in my hands. And for the record, my wife is not always right!

I am going to guide you and teach you how to simply build your own **Signature Swing** naturally, from the ground up. Throughout the process you will learn how to develop your own instinct and feeling for the movements that were made to fit your body like a glove, propelling your golf as far as you are willing to take it. You will learn the secrets that the golfing greats have known for generations and how the ball is ultimately your best teacher.

I have left the best till last; ***you can do all of this on your own.*** Yes that's right, without a little "wizard" constantly firing running commentary over your shoulder. There are many golfing gods that cherish every opportunity to make "simple" sound like a full blown symphony when actually the only trumpet that they are blowing is their own. Don't look any further. You are in the right place at the right time; your golf is now in safe hands! Please get yourself ready to have your little cotton golfing socks blown clean off. It gives me great pleasure to fight my corner, wiping the eyes of the guys looking through the rose-tinted glasses pushing and pulling your swing around like the school bully. Let's get in there and get the job done!

www.golfswingzone.com

Signature Golf Swing: Stop fighting with complicated swing mechanics!

As is often the case, the instructions detailed throughout this book refer to right-handed golfers, so for left-handed players please use a mirror image version. I have tried not to continually refer to you in the masculine form, so as not to offend any of you ladies out there, but I must confess that this has not always been possible. However my advice is phrased, it is aimed at all golfers without exception.

Lee Kopanski
Head (British) PGA Professional

Swing Myth Demolition

If you have never played golf before and these are your first steps, I want to make you aware of the golfing myths that walk the fairways of every golf course in the world. If you are already a seasoned golfer, I want to bring to your attention the fact that some of the advice or techniques that you have learned or heard of are totally wrong and extremely misguided. Some of these are taught and recommended by golfers who do not understand how your body works best and who are more interested in looking and sounding good rather than in the development of your golf career. The majority of these so called "quick fixes" or "magic swing thoughts" are pie in the sky that sneak past the untrained eye like a slippery snake loaded with poisonous venom, ready to kill your golf game stone dead. One slip up and the razor sharp teeth of your **Golf Swing Danger Zone** are patiently waiting to bite to the bone at the speed of light.

I am about to demolish the swing myths that are believed as key and fundamental to a great golf swing by many. I have seen many of these ideas in golf magazines and other golf literature that have brainwashed so many golfers into believing that they will change their golf for the better. The little experts are plentiful and are roaming the fairways, waiting to suck the life out of the vulnerable with their useless tips and tricks that are handpicked from the land of the fairies.

Golf can be dangerous even though it's not a contact sport, particularly if you are wrapping a golf club around your neck whilst standing on your head. Fighting through a mass of swing mechanics and technical details will not help you to untie the knots in your swing, but will rather prod and pick at your swing until it finds your weakest link. It is your responsibility to know what you are doing so that you can filter out the gold from the garbage, the butt stops here.

I have personally tried all of these swing myths myself and am about to save you from wasting a lot of precious time and energy drilling them into your bones. If you are advised to use any of these swing myths then my advice would be to politely say thank you and then walk away. If the advice is persistently unshakable and perched constantly firing running commentary over your shoulder, forget the small talk and run a four minute mile.

To trust your golf, place it into the hands of a PGA Professional

Swing Myth 1: Swing on the line of your target

If you didn't already know then you are about to find out that this game of golf that gives you extraordinarily addictive highs one moment only to drag you back down to earth by the scruff of your neck the next is an *explosive, target orientated sport*, different to no other. In other words it is just like tennis, football or throwing a ball to a distant target where you are pushed to your physical limitations. In golf, as with any other explosive sport, you will need to use your whole body *to the max* to truly get the best from yourself.

This is normally where all of the excuses start to flow out of the mouth of the golfer with no time to practise, two new hips or knees, a bad back or a full set of golf clubs that don't suit his/her game. I understand that we are all at different stages in life and all have our own set of problems to deal with but if you approach the game of golf with a slightly different attitude it will give you so much more back in return.

Many golfers that I meet have either come to the conclusion themselves or have been totally mislead into believing that a golf swing is swung in a straight line; back away from the target and back again in the direction of the target. At first it sounds quite logical to the untrained eye or from the mouth of the guy with all the answers, wearing rose-tinted glasses. I am about to prove to you that this little gem is a total myth that could be the cause of many of your nightmares on the fairways and the painful aftermath screaming at your bones, often lasting more than a day or two.

Throwing a ball is something that the majority of us can do with our eyes closed, without wondering where our arms and legs are during the throw, so that's where I am going to start in order to prove my theory. Throwing a ball is also an explosive, target orientated movement that uses the whole of your body to transfer the natural forces created during the throw to propel the ball on its way. Surprisingly this movement uses the same major muscle groups as a well-executed golf swing.

Firstly let's try and throw a ball in the same way as the guy that swings his golf club up and down on the line of the target. If your target is within easy reach and only a few metres away then this is the obvious and most accurate option. You draw your ball hand back away squarely from your target and then simply try to stay on this line to release the ball to your target during the throw. Push your target back fifty meters, however, and this blows this swing myth out of the sky. Now you need power, so where do you get it from, your hand and arm?

Signature Golf Swing: Stop fighting with complicated swing mechanics!

Backward movement throwing a ball on the line of the target   Forward movement throwing a ball on the line of the target

Chipping is a department of the golf game that requires little power but lots of feeling from your hands and arms to accurately control your shot. However, if you are swinging on the line of your target in your full golf swing then you are only using the small muscles in your hands and arms. You are losing the majority of your strength which comes from the use of your whole body. If this rings a bell then on an average par four you'll need at least six shots to make it to the fore-green and even Popeye would need three or four. If this is how you want to play the game then great, don't let me stop you. If you want to improve however, and I mean by a lot, you have to understand how the "boss" of your golf swing, your swing *direction* works.

Please don't take this personally. I understand that if this game is new to you then you won't know how it all works. If you are a seasoned golfer that has played for years then it's about time you stopped stamping your feet, pointing the finger and blaming your driver for its poor performance. The direction of a swing in golf is no different to that of the majority of other explosive, target orientated sports, obviously with the exclusion of just a few minor technicalities naturally characteristic of the sport or movement in question.

So how do you throw a ball to a target where the distance involved requires more force?

Set up

Firstly, when throwing a ball, you automatically stand in such a way that your ball (and *not your body*) is lined up with your target. By doing this you are giving yourself the best chance of hitting your target with your ball. You do not think about how your shoulders/hips/big toe are aligned in relation to your target, your focus is on ensuring that your *ball* is in line with your target.

Throw set up position   Golf address position

You naturally stand side on, *parallel* to the "ball to target line" (the line which runs from your ball to your target). This is no different as to how you should address your ball in golf. Aligning your *body* to the target, rather than your *ball* to the target (with your body parallel to this line) is a mistake that I encounter time and again.

www.golfswingzone.com

Drawing your ball back

Your target is your main point of focus. Your ball hand moves back behind your body and inside of your ball to target line. As it does so your body weight moves onto your right side.

Correct backward movement in a powerful throw

Correct backswing movement in a powerful golf swing

The combination of the direction of your ball hand and your weight transference naturally rotates your body. This is the same way a correctly executed backswing is performed. The swing direction aided with the weight transference onto your right side rotates your body.

If your ball hand was drawn back exactly on the line of your target your arm would disconnect away from your body and your rotation would be very limited. Your backswing is identical. If in your backswing your club head remains on the ball to target line your hands and arms are forced to disconnect too steeply away from your body. This has a knock on effect, restricting your weight transference and resulting in limited body rotation.

If this is your backswing your body weight favours your left leg and your hips are forced to slide across onto your right side. Your left knee is forced to collapse, your left shoulder drops and your head loses height. I have just described one of the most lethal golf swing cocktails known to man, a "Reverse Pivot", and this is only the beginning of why this swing myth is a total scam.

Incorrect backward movement for a powerful throw

Incorrect backswing movement in a golf swing resulting in a **reverse pivot**

Attacking your target

From the position behind your body your ball hand has to get back to your target line. To get back on track to the ball to target line your ball hand starts its forward motion moving to the right, to recover from the inside position created by drawing your ball back. Your body weight is smoothly transferred across to your left with your ball hand heading back in the direction of your target. Your weight transference and hand and arm direction combined rotates your body.

Signature Golf Swing: Stop fighting with complicated swing mechanics!

Correct angle of attack; powerful throw   Correct angle of attack; powerful golf swing

This is identical to a well-executed downswing that correctly attacks the ball from an inside downswing path. To get back on track to the ball to target line your club head starts its forward motion moving to the right to recover from the inside position created by your backswing. Your body weight is smoothly transferred across to your left with your club head heading back in the direction of your target. Your weight transference and swing direction of your club head combined rotates your body.

Releasing the ball

This is the half way stage of the throw. Your body weight is favouring your left side and your ball hand has met the ball to target line shortly before release. Your ball hand continues from here, heading in the direction of your target. Your weight transference to the left and ball hand direction naturally aid the rotation of your body further. As your ball hand arm reaches full extension you release the ball to your target.

Correct throw on target line   Correct golf swing impact and early follow through

This is identical to a correctly aligned and well-co-ordinated impact position in a golf swing. Your body weight favours your left side and your club head meets the ball to target line shortly before impact. Your club head continues from here, heading in the direction of your target. Your weight transference to the left and your swing direction naturally aid the rotation of your body further. As your arms reach full extension you hit your ball.

Momentum to the finish

After release your ball hand maintains its path heading towards your target for as long as physically possible. Your weight transference is complete with the majority of your body weight favouring your left side. Your weight transference and ball hand direction completes the rotation of your body. The momentum and complete rotation naturally pull your ball hand inside, off the ball to target line, to finish wrapped around your body.

www.golfswingzone.com

A well balanced finish to a throw   A well balanced finish to a golf swing

This is identical to a well-balanced follow through and finish position in a golf swing. Following impact your club head maintains its path, heading towards your target as far as physically possible. Your weight transference is complete with the majority of your body weight favouring your left side. The momentum and complete rotation naturally pulls your club head inside, off the ball to target line. Your hands finish over your left shoulder and your club shaft runs down your back.

End result

As you can see a powerful, well aligned throw in relation to a target is no different to a strong and accurate golf swing or for that matter to the majority of explosive, target orientated sports that are played from one side of the world to the other. It is now obvious that neither a throwing action nor a golf swing create power or use the full potential that your body weight and rotation add to the equation when throwing/swinging exclusively back and forth on a continuous target line. A golf swing that is swung on a line parallel to your target is therefore weak and more dangerous than you could ever imagine. The steep backswing that it produces destroys your co-ordination and forces your body out of its natural position. Your hands and arms disconnect away from your body leaving you wide open to a range of poor golf shots and vulnerable to pain from top to toe every time you play.

Incorrect backswing movement in a golf swing resulting in a **reverse pivot**

As you proceed into your downswing you are therefore starting out of position and are forced to either inconsistently compensate by looping back or to chop across your ball. The steep backswing position sets your hands and arms in a position too far away from your body. Looping back in order to correct your poor, steeply disconnected backswing produces a golf swing that you'll never trust in a month of Sundays, pulling and pushing your body around like a rag doll. By the time you have finished your round of golf you'll look like you've been dragged through a hedge backwards!

Your only other option in an attempt to get back on line to hit your ball is to have your hands and arms work back towards your body. Your downswing path is therefore starting too far outside of plane, cutting across and blocking your body at impact and finishing too far inside of plane (too far to the left of your target). Usually your hands and arms will finish wrapped too low around your body.

An outside to inside downswing path resulting in a blocked body and weak golf swing

The swing that I have just described is the chopping motion that produces numerous poor golf shots, ranging from a slice to a pull hook; I won't mention the other ten. Cutting across your body with this style of swing is the best way to find your weakest link, teasing your discs until you find yourself flat on your back in the middle of the driving range. You'll be looking up at the circle of sticky beaks that have gathered to have a nose and find out what's going on! I will cover this in greater detail later in **Golf Swing Danger Zone**.

The boss of your swing

An explosive, target orientated sport has a target. If you have a target then your *swing direction* is the boss of your swing. If the swing direction is poorly aligned in relation to your target you don't just miss, you are starting a chain reaction of events that run through your whole body.

Stand up and mimic your golf swing, simply swinging your hands and arms straight back and too, parallel to your target or too far to the right or left. You will feel your body being pushed and pulled around by the boss. If your swing direction is wrong in relation to your target then your weight transference and rotation is pulled with it. On the other hand if your swing direction is correctly aligned to your target your body will react accordingly and be guided naturally into the correct position. Trying to isolate and perfect your rotation in front of the driving range mirror has absolutely no effect and improves nothing. The only thing you can say that you have achieved is perhaps a stretch, but often with poor form.

A great player knows that when he starts misfiring (after firstly establishing that his set up is correct), then his swing direction must be his first port of call since this is the piece of framework that holds his swing together. Until you fully understand how a correct golf swing is directed in relation to your target you cannot even contemplate building your swing. A powerful golf swing revolves around its target, guided by the direction of its swing path. The weight transference to the right in the backswing and then to the left in the forward swing, guided by the swing direction rotates your body.

You can now clearly see that the power of any physical movement using the strength of your whole body comes from weight transference and rotation. This is guided to your target by the boss of the movement which is the direction in which you want to hit, punch, kick or throw. A powerful, consistent golf swing is therefore not swung in a straight line towards your target. This is totally misguided information from someone who has no idea how your body works best or is not interested in your improvement.

You will soon be armed with the knowledge to build your own individual **Signature Swing** exclusively with your own two hands and the wonderful piece of kit lodged between your ears. It's simple, yet very effective and uses your body in the way it was designed to move and instinctively react. You don't need your helpful friend sat perched on your shoulder firing out running commentary through his rose-tinted glasses any more. You can do this on your own, I promise.

So my friend, the choice is yours. If you want to continue to turn a par four into a par ten by swinging back and forth on the ball to target line then be my guest. If not don't allow this swing myth to cross your mind again!

To trust your golf, place it into the hands of a PGA Professional

Swing Myth 2: Keep your head down and still

This little old chestnut has destroyed many a good swing and totally blown to bits many a bad swing leaving only rubble in its trail of devastation. Go down to your local driving range and you'll hear this little gem of advice rolling off the tongues of those wizards of little knowledge. It is an understatement to say this is bad for a golf swing and an understatement to say that it might hurt from time to time. Little knowledge in any department in life is dangerous, this baby has the potential to put you flat on your back on a hospital trolley awaiting the results of your scan, so be warned. If you think I am being slightly rude by expressing myself in this way just wait until you get your hands on the guy that shouts "keep your head down and I'll watch your ball," one day he'll be enemy number one.

If anyone advises you to keep your head still and/or down, or holds a golf club shaft to your head to make a point of this then run a four minute mile. This is a great sign that they don't know what they are talking about or they just want to palm you off as fast as possible with a load of rubbish so they can get home and put their feet up in front of the television with a bag of crisps. If you stick with this helpful hint for any length of time you'll just make matters a hundred times worse.

I can't tell you the amount of times I've been told by pupils as they have hit a bad shot that they have lifted their head or that they were looking up too soon. Please forget it; this is not your problem. If you were playing tennis or football would your coach grab your hair or hold a stick to your head and tell you not to move it? If he were to, you would think he was crazy. In golf anything goes, I don't know why but it does and everyone's an expert, often with good intentions but little clout.

I am often asked by beginners where they should look, which is a perfectly reasonable question to start with. At your ball, of course! I often answer jokingly that if you look at your right foot, then you might just hit it... Golf is a dead ball sport and the difficulty lies in how you should play the ball which is something I will cover in depth later. Your ball isn't moving, it is waiting to be hit. Your brain functions best when reacting to a ball that is moving, rather than one waiting to be hit. This is a fact which has been scientifically proven and is not coming from the mouth of a simpleton like me but from those science boffins with big foreheads, so don't worry. It is totally logical if you compare a golf shot to catching a ball, how did you catch it? You didn't think about it did you? The boffins are right! In a dead ball sport we have more time to analyse the whole thing and to complicate it. Another thought provoking idea, try and hit a nail on the head with a hammer. Where do you look? Hopefully not at your finger!

The classic head down, head still pupil that I am often confronted with firstly addresses the ball with their eyes fixed firmly on the ball so intensely that they start burning a hole into it just like Superman can, I can smell the smoke. The address position generally looks tense. The backswing begins all with the hands and arms as they try so hard to keep their head perfectly still.

Keeping your head down and still generally leads to a tense address position

A tense backswing which is dominated by the hands and arms

www.golfswingzone.com

Signature Golf Swing: Stop fighting with complicated swing mechanics!

As they progress into their backswing their body is blocked from turning due to the strong determination to keep their head down and still. As they get to the top of the backswing their body weight hasn't transferred across onto their right side as it should and they are now pivoting over their left leg. Unbeknown to the pupil their endless struggle to keep their head perfectly still changes their spine angle. Their left knee collapses, their left shoulder drops and their head drops. This slides their hips over to the right for a reverse pivot of the finest order.

Turning over the left leg which results in a **reverse pivot**

They are now sat right in the middle of their **Golf Swing Danger Zone** which is waiting to bite like hell the moment they let their guard down. This little beauty is lovingly reinforced by all of the misguided but well-meaning dribblers perched ranting on over their shoulder, firing out running commentary which sounds a little like this, "Keep your head down and don't forget still." My poor pupil, their nightmare continues!

As they start their downswing their head has already noticeably dropped which is honed in on by all of their friends. "You're dipping again", but they struggle on! As they reach impact a massive effort is made to stay focused on the ball and even better, they call on the advice of their friends again. "Don't look up, stay down even when the ball has gone, we'll look for it." Their eyes remain pinned to the ground as they ask "where did it go?" Normally, not very far!

Attacking the ball from outside of plane with resulting loss of height   Eyes pinned to the ground in a huge effort to keep the head down and still   Resulting blocked follow through with body weight favouring the right side

This is not only the best way to play exceptionally poor golf but it's also the fastest way into an Accident and Emergency Room for treatment to your busted back. If you have a weak link this is the best way to find it. In pinning your eyes to the ground your head is not allowing your body to naturally turn into your follow through. Your swing finishes in an abrupt, jerky attempt to regain your composure and look like the golfer you want to be. If you are doing this it is only a matter of time until you pay the price by abruptly finishing your golf career and don't think that I'm exaggerating here. I've seen this time and time again. If you think I have a bee in my bonnet as I'm writing this I wouldn't like to see your face the day your luck runs out. It's not a very pleasant sight but a head on collision like this is always good business for your local physiotherapy team.

If you were to throw a ball you wouldn't think about keeping your head still, it would probably be as quiet as it should be. In tennis, as you return a serve, do you keep your head still? You don't even think about it but it must be reasonably still to balance your body. If you were to kick a football correctly your head would naturally be over your body. The moment your head falls back, your weight shifts onto your heels and you sky rocket the ball into the stands.

Your brain is the heaviest organ in your body. If your head moves too much your body either follows suit or has to compensate in some way to regain balance. Golf is no exception. What I am trying to say is that you shouldn't think about keeping your head still. If your golf swing is in reasonable condition and your swing direction is in good shape then you don't need to worry about your head. As in football or tennis your head will move as it should in your golf swing. Often this is noticeable with good players as a side to side movement which complements the natural weight transference that creates the power in their swings.

If you are often told by your friends that your head is bobbing about like an apple in a bowl of water, then don't look to your head to solve your problems. Your head is not the problem; the culprit is most probably your wild swing plane which is pushing and pulling you all over the place like a rag doll. The knock-on effect is a blocked rotation that the untrained eye of the beholder will see and try to quick fix. One thing is for sure; it's not your head, no matter how big it is...

What should you do?

- At address focus on a small area on the back of your ball that you want to make contact with. In your backswing stay focused on this point
- As you swing down maintain your focus on the ball

- Impact is normally a blur as your ball leaves your club head
- Allow your body to turn your head naturally out of the shot

- Finish your swing with your head well balanced over your body, admiring your great shot

There are great players that rotate their heads freely as they begin their downswing and don't look at the ball as they swing down but rather at a point between their ball and the target. I have tried this and trained on this, but have found it to be of no help whatsoever to me and pretty scary to boot, but never say never as every case is different. I don't promote this and don't recommend this; normally this kind of idiosyncrasy cannot be taught or learned and is generally a natural part of someone's make up.

So there we go. I hope you've got the message. If your motto is no pain no gain and you want to perfect weak and dismal golf shots then keep your head perfectly still and don't look up. At least you will be able to scrutinise your deep wedge of a divot that will be big enough to fill a bunker. Please don't forget that you have been warned; they're your bones you're busting…

To trust your golf, place it into the hands of a PGA Professional

Swing Myth 3: Hitting down on the ball

What are you trying to achieve here? Do you want to hit your ball into the ground? For a start your golf swing doesn't end at the ball but if you smash down at your ball long and hard enough you are going to hit the ground hard in more ways than one.

I don't understand the method behind the madness of hitting down at your ball. How can it encourage a positive effect on a golf shot? When you hit down at the ball you hit the ball and what then? The golf swing is called a swing for a reason, do you want to rename it and call it a dig, and dig a big hole for your golf career to jump straight into, because that's what you're doing?

Hitting down on the ball to dig a hole for your golf career to topple into…

Have you ever wondered why your hands, wrists, elbows, shoulders and back are causing you problems if you are hitting consciously down at your ball? Don't look any further. I know you have been taught this because I hear this from golfers time and time again. It's about time that you heard the truth. If you are advised to hit down on the ball again do yourself a favour and find somebody who knows what they are talking about and stop spending your free time with people who are filling your head with this reckless advice.

If you start your downswing hitting down on the ball then you are doing this with your hands, arms and upper body hitting at your ball. I would like to make you aware that this is a big no, no and is where your battle begins with loops that a cowboy would be proud of.

Hitting down on the ball with your hands, arms and upper body

Your downswing in golf, as in tennis or even when you throw a ball is started firstly by the transference of body weight moving across to your left, always firstly from your lower body. This shouldn't be something that you are conscious of; it is something that you will do naturally when all of the basics are in place. When you throw a ball you are not thinking about transferring your body weight. If you are, you're not the type of bloke/gal to win a cuddly bear for your better half on Blackpool promenade, so stay clear and don't make a fool of yourself

When a boxer throws a punch believe it or not, he throws it from his legs. That's where the phrase "fancy footwork" originates from. If his body weight wasn't transferring across, beginning with his lower body, then the punch, even if it landed, wouldn't carry any clout and would be of little benefit, whether faced with an amateur or the great Muhammad Ali. The problem, as I have already explained, is that golf is a dead ball sport and this can be a disadvantage. When you throw a ball or react to a ball many of the things that a golfer thinks about during their golf swing happen naturally during the throw or hit. The game of golf gets in your head because you have time to think about what your backside or big toe is up to. You don't need to know, it's not going to help your golf swing.

Hitting from the top of your backswing with your hands and arms down on the ball is the reason that you hit a wide range of embarrassing golf shots. In doing this you have been advised to improve your golf in a useless way and have wasted your time and energy doing so. In fact it would have been better to have stayed off the driving range and got involved in something more productive with your time like fishing or jogging. Why? You are programming your body to remember and repeat this rubbish, so stop digging your own golfing grave.

What do you think happens to your clubface as you smash it into the ground? If you hit the ground firmly the club will spin in your hands, opening or closing it. You will have no control over this which I think is quite important for you to know as the angle of your clubface has a big say in where your ball will end up. How do you hope to accelerate through your shot into your finish position? You won't! Your club head will be stuck in the ground with a follow through leaving you looking like you are walking on hot coals and not liking it, in a last ditch attempt to regain a little aesthetic composure. If you have hit down on your ball then at some stage you will have to swing back up in order to finish your swing. This is the big snag that is not fully understood by the many that are strongly promoting that you should hit down on your ball. In doing this you are losing all of the momentum that you have created in your swing which is absorbed by the ground that has been so well manicured for your enjoyment. If you continue on your quest to hit down on your ball you will be the green-keeper's nightmare and will be banned from playing on the course until the main events of the season are over. Although I know that you have been taught to do this, it simply doesn't work so stop hitting down on your ball because it is bad for your health and isn't doing your golf clubs any favours either...

Signature Golf Swing: Stop fighting with complicated swing mechanics!

Natural weight transference in a correct golf swing

Natural weight transference in a correct forehand tennis shot (from standing)

Natural weight transference in a powerful throw (from standing)

Hitting down on the ball throws all of your energy and momentum into the ground, remember what goes up must come down but what goes down doesn't always come back up. Keep doing this and I'm afraid to say that you're going down with it, my friend.

To trust your golf, place it into the hands of a PGA Professional

Swing Myth 4: The straight left arm

Keep your left arm perfectly straight and you'll be fine, what can go wrong from here? If your left arm is breaking down during any stage of your swing it is nothing to do with your arm. So stop forcing your arm to do something it doesn't want to do, it will hate you for it and the day will come when it makes you scream out in public. If you are lead to believe that this is your main swing fault or that to straighten your left arm is the answer then you are in the wrong place at the wrong time listening to the wrong advice.

The golf club is naturally rotated around your body by your hands and arms. If for some reason your hands and arms disconnect from your body, the collapse of your left arm is the obvious but often misunderstood flashing indication that something has gone wrong. When you have a cold most people get a red nose, however this is a symptom and not the cause. Please look past your nose! If you don't you could be introducing your arm to golfer's elbow, which if you have never heard of you certainly don't want to suffer from!

Your arm is a symptom of your swing fault. Slapping a plaster on it, as is often recommended, is bad news for your golf. I don't know any other sport where forcing your arm into a straight position has a positive outcome and I don't know why "keep your left arm straight" is heard so often on the fairways.

The classic straight left arm pupil stands to the ball and snaps his arm into a locked, straight position. As he does so a bead of sweat runs down his forehead. His set up looks stiff and tense as he tells himself that there's no way the arm is going to break this time. The swing is over in a flash with a quick chopping motion nearly cutting the ball in two.

The left arm forced into a straight position at address

He now turns to look at me and says "you see, there it is again straight right, but at least my left arm felt straight this time". Be my guest and try and convince him that it's nothing to do with his left arm, all his friends have a stiff left arm and Tiger Woods plays with a straight left arm. If you are him stop pointing your finger at your left arm. If you continue doing this your body will be so tense that it will not be allowed to turn freely, totally blocking your swing. You will chop the ball or pull hook the ball. You will be able to play every shot in the book but you won't know what's coming next. Exciting though, isn't it?! Generally the collapse of your left arm is down to a problem with your swing path direction (swing plane). If your backswing is too steep and your arms disconnect from your body your left arm will collapse. Forcing your left arm into position only adds to the problem.

Collapse of the left arm due to the hands and arms steeply disconnecting away from the body; target view

Collapse of the left arm due to the hands and arms steeply disconnecting away from the body; side view

Signature Golf Swing: Stop fighting with complicated swing mechanics!

If your downswing is too far to the left of your target your left arm will wrap itself around and behind your body. Your left arm then has no choice other than to collapse. The left arm breaking down is not your problem; please stop treating it as so.

Collapse of the left arm due to the downswing being directed too far to the left of the target; target view

Collapse of the left arm due to the downswing being directed too far to the left of the target; side view

Many golfers are not flexible enough to maintain a straight left arm and as they get to the top of their backswing have a bend in their left arm. This is not a problem; don't fight with it any longer. If you look more closely at some of the best players in the world I think you will be surprised.

So what's all the fuss about and why is this golden nugget of knowledge ingrained into so many golfers? A wide swing arc is a key ingredient in the production of a powerful golf shot, as the wider the swing arc the more weight that there is on the outside of the arc which generates increased club head speed. I believe that this is where the obsession with the straight left arm begins. I can't argue with that as a wide swing arc does create power, but manufacturing a straight left arm rather than concentrating on the basic ingredients (fundamentals) won't cause your soufflé to rise.

To trust your golf, place it into the hands of a PGA Professional

Swing Myth 5: Low and slow

Low and slow is great advice if you want to learn how to swing around your ankles in your backswing. If you combine this with "keep your head down and still" or "straight left arm" you will be lucky to hit a fairway all day.

At some point or other "low and slow" has been in every golf magazine or DVD in every available language and is highly recommended as a great way to start your swing. "Brush the grass as you start your backswing" is a classic or you will be told to place a tee in the ground behind your ball and be taught to make contact with it as you swing away from your ball. Your arms are only so long. Using this poor advice you will start to reach out with your hands and arms in a struggle to maintain them low and slow, resulting in pulling your body and spine out of their natural position. What happens when you reach out? Your left knee collapses, your left shoulder drops, your head drops and you start to pivot/turn over your left leg. This is the perfect recipe for a well-executed reverse pivot which is one of the biggest golf swing killers of all time. A reverse pivot is not good for your bones in any way, shape or form and will wreck your golf swing so stop listening to this terrible advice.

A typical low and slow pupil will make a few practice swings, brushing the grass back until the club head runs out of driving range behind him. As he takes his backswing away he takes every mole hill or clump of grass with him which he explains is the only disadvantage. "It's not quite as smooth as I'd like it to be." In doing so his arms are not long enough to follow the correct swing path so he starts to swing in behind his body until it's not possible to keep his club head to the ground anymore. His body has now turned too far, too early and totally out of sequence. Bingo! A solid foundation on which to build a beautiful reverse pivot!

Correct address position; target and side view

The club head forced to remain in contact with the ground

The backswing turned too early, totally out of sequence into a flat position forcing the body weight onto the left leg

His backswing is now much too flat (inside/under plane) so he now makes a remarkable effort to compensate for this with a steep rise of his hands and arms like he did at school when he knew the answer. At the same time his hands and arms disconnect cleanly from his body as his body buckles down over his left leg.

The hands and arms steeply disconnecting away from the body

Now this is the best bit of his explanation, "but it's my right shoulder again" as he starts his downswing, "I'll have to hold it back a bit" he tells me. He believes that his perfectly healthy right shoulder is his biggest downfall, a fact that all of his friends are eager to point out.He has now taken his backswing in behind his body. From there his hands are hoisted straight up to the sky. Now get ready for the part that any cowboy with his lasso would be proud of, with the aid of this great combination of events and the momentum in his swing he produces a beautiful loop in a last ditch attempt to get back to the ball. His downswing is now attacking his ball from a position too far away from his body. He is now heading back towards and across his body, totally blocking what was left of the little rotation he managed to achieve.

Signature Golf Swing: Stop fighting with complicated swing mechanics!

This is known in the trade as an Out-In downswing path set up by a low and slow reverse pivoting backswing. A classic swing style to stay clear of!

The downswing attacking the ball from a position too far outside of plane, finishing too far inside of plane, swinging to the left of the target; target view

The downswing attacking the ball from a position too far outside of plane, finishing too far inside of plane, blocking the rotation of the body; side view

If this is how you want to make your way around the golf course you will be pleased to know that this will help you to Slice, Pull, Pull Hook, Top or hit a divot that would fill a bunker.

If anyone tells you that your right shoulder is the problem, holds your shoulder or tries to get you to block its movement in some way, take an early shower! The shoulder is the red nose you get with a cold, a symptom and not the cause of the problem. Your hands, arms and body are connected. If you were to throw your hands and arms away from your body as if you were to start your downswing your shoulder would be naturally pulled with it!

Low and slow is not good for much as you have seen so please, if this is you, stop ranting on about your right shoulder in your downswing. Your shoulder is not your problem, your low and slow backswing is. If you keep doing this you won't play low but for sure you'll be slow!

To trust your golf, place it into the hands of a PGA Professional

Swing Myth 6: Pull down with your left hand

Trying to fix something by slapping a plaster on the problem as is often advised for your golf swing is a great cheat and an easy way out for the chap with all the answers. The one major problem is that you can't run away and hide from the problem, well certainly not fast or far enough without the plaster slipping off. Eventually your fault will catch up with you only to give you a big kick up the backside. Yes that's right, it works for a while and it might give you a boost until it leaves you eventually looking through your fingers.

Being told to pull your left hand down from the top of your backswing is a classic piece of useless advice that runs through many a club house locker room. Why, when you've got two hands, would you only want to use the power and control of one? Your hands, arms and body become disconnected due to your left hand dominating. When you are playing baseball or cricket do you hit the ball more with one hand than the other, especially when you are trying for a home run or a big six? If you pull your golf club down from the top of your backswing with your dominant left hand and stop at impact, your clubface is left wide open because your left hand is stronger than your unused right hand which naturally trails. Hit your ball this way and the only thing that will be left wide open for longer than a few seconds is your mouth in disbelief at how erratically you can play the game you love so much.

Pulling down with the left hand from the top of the backswing resulting in an open clubface at impact; side view

To be most effective your body parts should work naturally, in one harmonious movement. It doesn't make sense to try and artificially manufacture the transition phase or indeed any phase of your swing. If you want to create a constant fight for balance and control then please be my guest, but this does not work and is a sure fire sign that this is coming from someone who doesn't know what they are talking about. This bad piece of advice is often used to combat a slice (a ball flight which begins left of the target and curves strongly to the right) which is produced by an outside to inside downswing path problem, where a golfer initiates his downswing with his upper body. This is normally the result of a player that has poorly rotated in his backswing, resulting in his hands and arms disconnecting away too steeply from his body. He is basically fixing a fault with another fault only to slap a plaster on top. The plaster can only mask the problem for so long, after which you are left with a wide open clubface which doesn't really complement an outside to inside downswing path unless you want to hit a slice so big that your ball boomerangs back to you! Your clubface will be so far open that on a hot day you could fry an egg on it!

Pulling down with the left hand from the top of the backswing in a vain effort to bring the downswing back on plane, resulting in an open clubface at impact; target view

Most amateurs believe that their hips start their downswing or that they need to pull their left hand down from the top of their backswing or manufacture movements that make no sense. To really get the most out of yourself you need understand that golf is no different to any other explosive, target orientated sport. Just because the ball is not moving doesn't mean to say that the physical movements are different…

Push something, pull something, or lift something. Are you stronger or do you have more control with one hand? No! So stop believing that you do.

I look forward to introducing you to "The Power in Transition" later, and believe me it's got nothing to do with pulling down with your left hand…

To trust your golf, place it into the hands of a PGA Professional

Swing Myth 7: The Perfect swing

So have you found it then? I don't suppose you would be reading this if you had. I know you've probably already looked at books, DVD's and on the internet for your perfect golf swing. That's great! Which one is it then? Which swing is the one that's going to make the difference? It's like being a kid in a sweet shop or is it more like being a bull in a china shop?!

Let's take a quick look at what we have got to choose from. Is it the One Plane Swing (Rotary) the Two Plane Swing (Stack and Tilt) or even up and down the tree? Whatever takes your fancy! It is a mine field, I've been there myself. I've also tried to find the secret to this game and the fact of the matter is that there is no perfect swing.

If anyone tells you that there is a perfect swing or that they have found it they're not being honest with you. There are similarities in great swings which is why great swings work so well, because they have common traits that are fundamental to their success. If you are an average golfer you can learn a lot from the best players in the world. I do not doubt that for one minute, if you want to learn the most you learn from the best.

The problem starts when you see the image of Tiger Woods on one side of the screen and on the other side is the most important golfer in your world, you of course. I don't know you so maybe your golf is right up there with Tiger but let's assume that it is not, just yet. Tiger Woods is an athlete, he has a rock solid body that can consistently turn around itself at lightning speed, and has been able to do so virtually since the day he was born. I am not saying you're not fit or an athlete yourself; I am in reasonably good shape, but please don't compare me to Tiger Woods!

What I am trying to say is that if you play two or three times a week, have a full time job, keep fit when you get chance, have kids or a busy social life, don't try and swing like Tiger. If someone puts you up there on a screen alongside Tiger, ask them why they think that you should be compared to a player of his calibre. This is definitely a compliment! You can learn a lot from great players but you're not Tiger. Get over it and please don't let anyone even start to try to make such a comparison.

If you are a young and ambitious golfer reading this and want to be Tiger I think that is great, in fact I believe that's what life is all about, striving to be the best. Some great advice that I was given years ago which really helped me was being told to find my own swing, that works for me and to *master* it. Don't be stuck in the middle of one hundred swing thoughts every time you play. It doesn't work; I bear the scars to prove it and could sing a song or two about it. You need to get to know how your body feels and how your golf swing works best for you! You need a strategy that you can build from the ground up every time you play, whatever the conditions. I will take you there shortly!

Through the year I teach a lot of people. Everyone has something that glues their golf swing together. The problem with many amateurs is that they only come to me when they're about to hang up their boots, when they've tried everything else, all the quick fixes and have slapped as many plasters on their swings as possible. On the other hand a good player knows that he can learn a lot about what he is doing well when he is playing well.

Technique, in most sports, goes through one fashion to the next. A pupil of mine may have read something in a magazine about the Stack and Tilt, he decides this is the one for him; this is going to rock his golfing world, only to find out he has the same old problem.

There are many different ways to learn golf and to play golf, take the Stack and Tilt or the Rotary for example as these are two swings that have been in the headlines. The Stack and Tilt is a swing where your arms and shoulders swing on two different planes with your arms being steeper than your body whereas the Rotary is a one plane swing because your arms swing up to be approximately on the same plane as your shoulders.

Stack and Tilt; Backswing   Rotary; Backswing

There is nothing new about either of these swing styles. Jack Nicklaus has used the Stack and Tilt for generations and the great Ben Hogan used the Rotary swing for generations, both with great success. So get over all of this technical stuff, it's about time you learned to use the swing of the most important golfer on this planet, yours of course!

Why not find your own swing? Do you think that one day someone jumped out from behind a bush and shouted to Mr Nicklaus, "Hey Jack, try the Stack and Tilt it'll make you famous"? If you want to become good or improve, propelling yourself to your next level you have got to find out what works for you, with your own two hands!

If you want a perfect swing you will need to build a machine. Thankfully we are all human, all full of flaws and one thing is for sure, golf is not a game of perfection. If you find the perfect swing that fits every shape and size please let me know, I'm still looking for it. I want you to stop believing that there is a one-stop shop where you can buy the perfect swing. Why not master your own instead, using your own feeling and instincts? It's a lot easier to work with what you have, in the way that you were made. This is the secret that all the golfing greats have known for generations. I will show you how!

There are three more swing myths that I will be demolishing later as we start to build your swing:

Swing Myth 8: The Tiger Effect. I will give you a clue; it's quite hip.

Swing Myth 9: **Perfectly Still and 90** and I am not talking about your age.

Swing Myth 10: The Biggest Cock Up. The most over taught, over-analysed and destructive swing myth of them all. I am determined to put this one to bed for the last time.

I am sure these will open your eyes up once again and change the way you think about your golf swing, forever!

Over-analysis is unnecessary, if you perfect the basic fundamentals your body will automatically be in the right place at the right time and you won't be giving these myths a second thought!

To trust your golf, place it into the hands of a PGA Professional

Dynamic Foundation

To play golf consistently and to get the most out of yourself you need to be dynamically ready to fire into action, rather than comfortable or technically perplexed. Golf is underestimated and often not given the respect it deserves by the guy who has just blown his back to bits with the explosive part of the game he loves so much, treating the game as just a walk in the park.

Golf is an explosive sport; if you can get your head around it and start with this in mind you will be introducing your golf to a whole new ball game with a totally new spring in its step whatever your standard or stage in life. Just being comfortably positioned when you address your ball is not enough by anyone's standards. You need to be dynamically ready. By this I mean ready to go from your start position, athletically poised and free to perform under any set of conditions or circumstances.

Most amateur golfers are standing in their own way right from the very beginning, permanently fighting the after effects of a poor foundation, dancing from pillar to post, chasing their ball around the golf course, up and down dale, from one shot to the next.

If you want to build your swing correctly, dynamically from the ground up, then keep reading. If you want to eliminate the majority of your faults by learning how to find the correct position naturally tailored to your body, keep reading. If you want to continue carelessly and blindly throwing one quick fix after another at your golf, looking like a dog chasing its tail then may I give you forewarning; your golf career my end abruptly and it might not be pretty!!

With my simple techniques you will learn never to fight with Mother Nature; you can achieve great things with what you have. I'm afraid you've got what you were given so stop trying to be someone you're not. Hanging from a tree all night will not lengthen your arms by any significant amount. Why not try the natural way that fits the way you were made to walk this earth without placing yourself in a permanent head lock in an attempt to fight your way around the fairways? You will learn that simple is the key, by learning simple but effective methods that really make sense and work on the fairways in the real world. The days of tying yourself up in knots of technical jargon are about to be escorted off the premises, barred for life.

Get ready to breed confidence right through your game and to learn more about your body and what works best for you, using the hands of the most important golfer in your world. The hero in you is about to come out to play...

You are about to begin to learn how you can build your golf swing from the ground up, by yourself. Yes that's right, by yourself; you don't need anyone else, great isn't it? It is possible and I'm about to show you how. You can do it with just a little elbow grease, it is not complicated stuff to stay on top of, and it doesn't take years to master. Get ready to be open to new ideas loaded with powerful, easy to perform techniques that will tear through your game, propelling your golf all the way up to your **Top Gear**.

It never ceases to baffle me and if I'm honest, at times gets under my skin, just how complicated the beautiful game of golf is portrayed as being. A wise man once shared with me that the majority of people walk around town with their eyes closed and their hands over their ears, looking for the quickest way to the land of milk and honey. There is no express train out of here and certainly nothing comes to those who don't firstly know what they are doing. He did however state, with great passion and authority, that

"Often something complicated is something simple that is just not fully understood"!!

To trust your golf, place it into the hands of a PGA Professional

Clubface alignment: Don't just stab in the dark

Before we even get started here, never practise or play any target oriented sports without firstly establishing a target. Without a target you have no guide, leaving you stranded with nothing to learn. Your golf will be useless, a total stab in the dark. You need to develop feeling for your target as this is your ultimate goal, without it you are lost. How can you say that you have hit a good shot if you didn't have a target? Don't do anything until you have selected a target and certainly don't listen to the advice of someone who doesn't firstly recommend that you select a target as this is a sure fire sign they don't know what they are talking about!

Signature Golf Swing: Stop fighting with complicated swing mechanics!

The importance of correct clubface alignment in relation to your target is something which is often overlooked during the set up. If you consistently address your ball with a closed clubface pointing left of your target, it is amazing how fast this becomes second nature and part of your make-up. At first it may not be such a big issue but often the effects of your clubface being closed will gradually creep into your whole game shaking it from the roots up. Where does the average golfer point his finger when his ball is careering left into the woods? At his swing, of course! It's amazing how much compensation and dancing around that is involved in attempting to correct such a simple mistake!

So how do we make sure that your clubface is correctly aligned at address? This is a perfectly logical thought process that needs to be spot on for your ball to finish where you want it to. Believe me, this is one of the most crucial elements in your set up. The ball will normally finish where the clubface is aiming, regardless of what the rest of your swing or body is doing. If your clubface alignment is out, the ball will finish in the wrong place. The most important fundamental that runs through the veins of a consistent golf swing is that the clubface must be square in relation to the ball and target, throughout. If not, then you will never be able to trust your swing in a month of Sundays and you will never know what's coming next as you twist and turn, manoeuvring your body in an effort to compensate.

So in simple terms, if the clubface is open (aiming to the right of your target) your ball will finish it's flight to the right of your target. If the clubface is closed (aiming to the left of your target) the ball will finish it's flight to the left of your target. This should always be your number one check. A clubface alignment problem produces a golf swing that needs to move around, twisting and turning out of position, fighting to get your clubface back on line. The compensations you need to make to correct your clubface alignment will not serve you well for your first tee shot in your monthly medal but you might be the lucky winner of a prize on stage in a belly dancing contest. In simple terms you will never trust it...

This is how you correctly align your clubface to your target:

- Stand behind your ball
- Select and focus on your target
- Pick out a position on the ground approximately within a metre in front of your ball in your target line. (This could be a discoloured piece of grass or a piece of wood.)

    REMINDER: Do not touch this point with your hand or club head as you will be penalised!

- Focus on that point
- Align your clubface to this point

Standing behind the ball, selecting a point within one metre on the ball to target line

Why would you want to aim at a target that's three hundred metres away when you can align yourself to something that is only one metre away? If this is new to you it's probably something you've never even considered and you'll be surprised to know it is the same simple check that every great golfer has as part of his pre-shot routine. Do you believe that the great players of the modern game complicate the basics? Everybody gets nervous and feels pressure; the best way to retain composure is to keep it simple. If the best of the best are doing it, it can't be all bad, so make sure that this is your number one check.

Where does it all go wrong?

Most faults in a golf swing come from poor set up. If you have alignment problems you are leaving yourself wide open to a range of swing faults that will walk straight into your life. You will spend your whole golf career fighting and compensating for the simple mistakes that you are making before you have even taken your club away in your backswing. Many golfers are laying classic traps down unknowingly before their very own twinkle toes, toes which are ready and waiting to take the bait.

The Optical illusion

The biggest alignment problem is the way you see your target. If you stand directly behind your target facing it, it is much easier to align your body to it as both eyes are squarely fixed, which is the natural choice for you as we have hunted down our prey this way for centuries. This is the natural, balanced way that your brain works and processes the information standing before it best. As soon as you are side on to your target and address your ball things start to look differently. The right eye is more dominant as you turn and tilt your head to look at your target. Naturally this starts to mislead the brain as your head tilts to look at the target, bending your line of vision further to the right than it actually is. The problem lies in the eye of the beholder.

Viewing the target from face on

Viewing the target from side on at address

Off the rails

The second biggest classic amateur culprit with body alignment problems that I hear time and time again amongst club golfers occurs when you align your body to your target. I don't know why but many golfers actually believe that their body must be aligned to their target. When you play tennis or throw a ball do you align your body to your target? Never! So stop doing this when you are playing golf. If you are given this as advice, you are listening to someone who doesn't know what they are talking about or is not interested in the development of your golf. In other words run like the clappers, you're in the wrong place at the wrong time my friend. Aligning your body to your target for any shot that you play is one of the worst and most fatal mistakes that run through golf club locker rooms all over the world. For a start you are aiming in the wrong direction which is rather important to understand if you want to play your best golf. Then there are your precious bones which you are without a shadow of a doubt setting up for a high speed collision course of pain and devastation.

Aligning your body to the target is a common, yet very misguided mistake. At best, you will hit the ball to the right of your intended target because you have aligned your body, rather than your clubface, to the target. The best and simplest way to understand how aligning your body to the target is completely miles away from where it should be is to use the example of the rails of a train track. If your body is running parallel to the inside rail in line with your target, then the outside rail which the ball is sitting on is now running parallel to your body but to the right of your target! Oops!

Now it is as clear as day. So, my friend, it's about time you smelled the roses, got your head around it and dragged yourself out of this bad habit before your golf and your bones reap the consequences.

Signature Golf Swing: Stop fighting with complicated swing mechanics!

Incorrectly addressing the ball with the body aligned to the target

"V" bad compensation

Most golfers now think that they can simply get around this well-practised body alignment problem by aligning their clubface to the target. This solves absolutely nothing and just reinforces all of the bad stuff. To say it's wrong is an understatement, it is placing your golf and bones under undue stress from a totally careless mistake. Your body and clubface (which is now in a closed position in relation to your body) are aiming V shaped to your target.

Incorrectly addressing the ball with the body aligned to the target and
incorrectly compensating with the clubface also aligned to the target

Try running with both your feet pointing inwards in a V shape and you'll end up falling flat on your face. Guess what? You are placing your body in the same scenario in your golf swing! You cannot consistently compensate for poor body alignment. Your swing will be totally blocked and prevented from turning correctly, bringing your downswing, follow-through and golf career to an abrupt halt. If you play this way too often you will feel the stress attacking your lower back, firing a lightning bolt of pain straight into your bones, often leading to serious injury. So please be warned, your **Golf Swing Danger Zone** awaits you.

If you think that you're the type of Houdini guy that can make a great escape from this mess that you are wrapping yourself up in here, you could try and get yourself out of jail by swinging in the direction of your target. Your sub-conscious will know that your target is further to your left even if you don't. Your body will automatically try to compensate for this miscalculation by swinging your hands and arms across your body in an attempt to get your club head back to the target.

This is one of the most dangerous swing faults or as in this case compensations that your body could be forced to make. If you like your local back surgeon and you'd like to get to know him really well then this is mission nearly accomplished! You are chopping your body in two using only your hands and arms, with the end result being weak and inconsistent golf shots.

Initiating the downswing outside of plane, swinging to the left in a vain effort to bring the club head back to the target

Swinging too far to the left in a struggle to get the club head to the target

Completing a downswing which is blocking the weight transference onto the left side in turn inhibiting the body's rotation

The outside rail should run from your ball to your target. The inside rail now runs parallel to this, aligning your whole body, feet, knees, hips and shoulders to the left of your target.

Signature Golf Swing: Stop fighting with complicated swing mechanics!

A correctly aligned body and clubface in relation to the target

From this moment forward your clubface alignment will be your number one check. The benefits will amaze you as you simply align your clubface to your target. Stand back and watch your ball finish exactly where you want it to!!

Check 1: Be Square to One Metre

To trust your golf, place it into the hands of a PGA Professional

Grip pressure: Please don't release me or let me go!!

Don't be shy, I'm not going to ask you to stand up and sing, I just want you to stand up to some of the poor advice that has plagued your golf for so long. The biggest problem with grip pressure, believe it or not, is that too many players are taught that throughout their swing they should use soft hands, gently holding the golf grip for maximum power and control.

A golf grip that begins too relaxed will need to be adjusted during the swing. I know you are thinking that this is going against one of the golden rules of golf. This is the reason that at the top of your backswing you feel your grip slip and then you begin an almighty panic to quickly correct and compensate for it, often miles too late in order to get a good shot out there.

"Soft hands, easy grip", this is one of the leading swing thoughts causing clubface alignment problems in the golf swing. If you play tennis or baseball do you have a relaxed grip? No! Your grip is reasonably firm because you want to make good firm contact with the ball. Golf is no exception, so it's about time that the two wet fish that are holding your golf club firmed up a bit. It's a revolution in itself, after all the hours that the drill sergeant within you has spent putting you through your paces to crack this little gold nugget.

A classic piece of advice that has guided many golfers over the years came from the great Sam Snead who said that you should hold the club as if you had a little baby bird in your hands. Sam Snead is a legend, highly respected throughout the world of golf, but why would anyone want to hold their golf club with the same pressure as if they were holding a baby bird in their hands? I've never found myself holding a baby bird in my hands before, but I can imagine that you'd have to keep quite a tight hold or he'd fly away. Soft hands make for a pretty useless bird cage.

We are all individual; some stronger, weaker, faster or slower. So why do we all want to follow the same rules? What works for one man won't work for the next and I am a great believer that this is one mistake many a man has fallen for, myself included. Have you ever considered that maybe the legendary Sam Snead held the golf club too tightly in his hands? Perhaps to compensate for this he would imagine holding a cuddly delicate baby bird in his hands to prevent him from gripping the club too tightly, which would obviously then have helped him. I never had the pleasure of meeting the great man to ask him personally, but I hope that you can see my point here. What is soft and gentle to one man could be too firm and strong to the next for the baby bird to be able to catch its breath.

If you want to get the most out of your game you have to be yourself and find your own swing. You and only you will know if you are holding the golf club too tightly. If you are doing, it will be obvious in your swing which will look and feel full of tension. Your golf glove will be ripped to shreds and/or your golf grips worn to the bone with only a few games under their belt. You have to find somewhere in the middle that works for you.

Your grip pressure should be firm enough to maintain a consistent hold on your golf club throughout your entire swing. If you release the club in your hands during your swing due to the pressure being too light you will have to compensate by re-gripping, often too firmly, in a panic to regain control. If your grip pressure is too tight, then tension becomes a problem in your swing, running through and inevitably blocking your body, producing weak and inconsistent golf shots.

You are reading this to improve *your* golf. Stop comparing yourself and learn to develop your own feeling for what works well with your own two hands.

Check 2: Don't Release me or strangle me!

To trust your golf, place it into the hands of a PGA Professional

The Golf grip for your hands

There is more to your golf grip than meets the eye and without being armed with this knowledge your golf grip will be no different to the way that a child's splash painting is put together, colourful but terribly erratic and never to be produced the same way again. Before you start to even think about your grip it is imperative that you understand what you are trying to achieve with your grip and how you want it to position your body!

A good grip is designed to complement your swing. When set correctly at your address position a good grip will hold your swing together like glue. Your grip has a direct influence on the clubface and how it behaves in your swing. In my mind the key fundamental to a great swing is how you control the clubface. If you develop a clubface alignment problem due to a poor grip your body will have to move around, twisting and turning, dancing around all over the place in a mad attempt to compensate for it. A simple clubface problem, as we have already established, will drain you of all your energy as you spend most of your time fighting your way around the golf course.

The left arm and wrist as an extension of the golf club shaft

Gripping in the centre of the body breaks the extension of the left arm and golf club shaft which often results in a strong grip

I can't stress how important it is that your grip positions your left arm and wrist as an extension of your golf club. It is fundamental to the control of your clubface that your grip places your hands in a position on your golf club that naturally squares your left wrist position parallel to your arm. If your wrist position is not parallel to your arm or the wrist breaks down during the early stages of your backswing then your clubface will flap around opening and closing. If you overlook this simple golden rule your swing will never be consistent and will be impossible to trust. I will explain the full significance of this when we get on to the swing shortly.

The main reason that golfers find it difficult to achieve a solid straight left wrist position is because they are either not aware of the important role this plays or they grip the golf club in the centre of their body. If you take your grip from the centre of your body then the extension from your left arm to golf club will automatically be broken at the wrist. Try it for yourself; your wrist angle will no longer be square to your arm. This is one of the biggest culprits in causing a strong grip where your left hand is turned too far over showing too much of the back of your left hand as you look down. This often produces a ball flight that spins viciously to the left of your target.

The incorrect hand and wrist position also encourages far too much wrist hinging/cocking in your backswing which often leads to you fanning the clubface open, resulting in a weak ball flight spinning to the right of your target. You may think that these two wrongs make a right by balancing each other out but unfortunately a bar of chocolate wrapped in a lettuce leaf won't make you skinny. Your guess is as good as mine as to where your ball will finish but one thing is for sure, if this is you I wouldn't put my life on the line if you had to hit an island green surrounded by water. It all comes down to that word trust again, do you trust it?

This is too much information for now; firstly let's get your left hand on the grip so that your left arm and left wrist run as an extension of your club shaft.

Your left hand

- Stand tall, holding your club with your right hand at waist height, pointing to one o'clock
- The handle of the golf club runs from a point just above the bottom of your little finger and down through to the middle joint of your index finger
- Close your hand onto the grip of your golf club
- Your thumb should be slightly right of the handle. Please note that this is important as this thumb supports the club shaft during your backswing, especially at the top of the backswing.

Please don't position your thumb down the centre of the handle, this offers no support at the top of your backswing often resulting in the last three fingers of your left hand releasing from the handle. This inevitably leads to the handle slipping in your hands, resulting in an open or closed clubface as you start your downswing.

- The line between your index finger and thumb should now be pointing directly to the centre of your body
- As you lower the club head to the ground, if you look in a mirror (face on) you will now notice that your left arm and wrist are an extension of your golf club. I believe this to be a key fundamental for optimum control over your club head in every stage of your swing.

 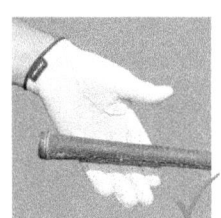 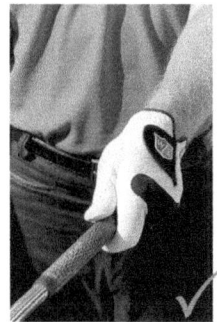 

How your right hand fits onto your grip is in your hands!

Depending on a number of individual factors there are three types of right hand positions. Your grip not only sets the hands and clubface squarely it is also where you will develop your feeling so it is highly important that you are happy with your grip of choice. I will guide you through the different variations but it is inevitably your decision that counts.

Your right hand should fit onto your handle to complement your left hand position as well as your left wrist and arm. Your grip will be so much more effective by not only bringing your hands together, working as one unit, but also by maintaining the relationship with your body during your swing. This will all come to light as we move onto the swing shortly.

Your Left hand is on the grip from waist height at one o'clock. Get ready for your right hand.

The Vardon Overlapping Grip

The Overlapping grip is the gold stamp of golf grips. The majority of Tour players use this grip due to the consistency that it offers. The Overlapping grip links the two hands together, firmly encouraging everything to work as one unit from start to finish. If your hands are fine and you don't have arthritic pain and your hands allow you to use the overlapping technique then this is the best choice of grip to complement your left hand. It offers a solid hold on to your golf club handle and your hands will incur less movement during your swing, in turn achieving superior control over your clubface.

The right hand Overlapping Grip continues as follows:

- Place the little finger of your right hand on top of the gap in between the index and middle finger of your left hand
- The thumb of your left hand fits neatly into the lifeline of your right hand
- The handle of your golf club fits neatly into the middle of the index finger of your right hand

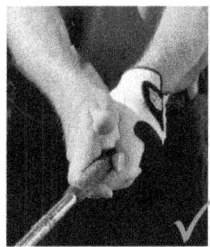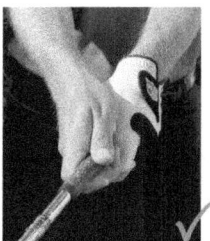

A great way to check if your right hand is on correctly is to check that the line between your index finger and thumb runs parallel to the line between the index finger and thumb of your left hand.

The Interlocking Grip

The Interlocking grip is the grip that Tiger Woods uses. I know that you're thinking well if it's good enough for him then it's good enough for me, right?! Tiger Woods doesn't have many problems with his golf, as we are all fully aware! However, he has always fought with his clubface alignment during his swing which I believe is a direct result of his choice of grip. If your hands are small or you have weak forearms and wrists the Interlocking grip may help you. The major downfall of this style of grip is that you run the risk of having the handle stray into the palms of your hands, producing an elongated thumb which is prone to slipping during your swing.

Both Jack Nicklaus and Tiger Woods use the Interlocking grip. I know that you're thinking who am I to tell you otherwise? Jack Nicklaus himself is on record as saying his only regret about his technique was that his hand size and shape did not allow him to use the Overlapping grip. Consequently his left thumb would often slip at the top of his backswing, causing his hands to separate a little.

The right hand Interlocking Grip continues as follows:

- Place the little finger of your right hand between the index finger and middle finger of your left hand
- The thumb of your left hand fits neatly into the lifeline of your right hand
- The handle of your golf club fits neatly into the middle of the index finger of your right hand

Signature Golf Swing: Stop fighting with complicated swing mechanics!

 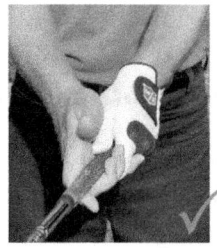 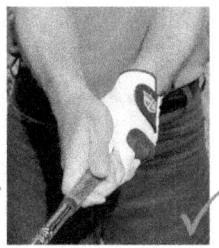

You can check if your right hand is on correctly in the same way for each of these three grips. Check that the line between your index finger and thumb runs parallel to the line between the index finger and thumb of your left hand.

The Baseball Grip

The Baseball grip carries all of the same risks as the Interlocking grip. The Baseball grip however does offer some advantages if you have problems with your hands. If you suffer with joint pain or arthritis or feel that your hands are weak or small then this is often the best alternative. Your hands fit onto your grip but without the linking of the little finger of your right hand. This makes it difficult to maintain a compact hand position on the grip during your swing. It's not all bad, some great players have won some big tournaments using the Baseball grip and again I wouldn't like to argue with them.

The right hand Baseball grip continues as follows:

- Place the little finger of your right hand against the index finger of your left hand
- The thumb of your left hand fits neatly into the lifeline of your right hand
- The handle of your golf club fits neatly into the middle of the index finger of your right hand

 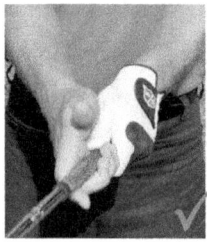 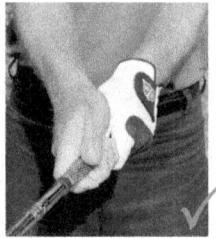

Once again you can check if your right hand is on correctly by checking that the line between your index finger and thumb runs parallel to the line between the index finger and thumb of your left hand.

To summarise, your choice of grip is totally down to you and your personal preferences. The one point that I can't stress enough is that the main importance of the grip is to bring your left hand, left arm and wrist square, running as an extension of the golf club shaft. This sets the clubface square at address and allows your backswing to start correctly. It is also important to note again that as you take your grip you should always do so from the one o'clock position as this naturally sets your left hand, left arm and wrist correctly.

Check 3: Grip in line at one o'clock for a straight left wrist

To trust your golf, place it into the hands of a PGA Professional

Posture: Alive and kicking

Bring your swing to life; get out of your own way and your golf will be "Alive and Kicking". You should be comfortable when you go for a walk in the park or when you lie in bed at night, to get a good night's sleep, but should you get comfortable before you throw your body into an explosive sport? Golf is an explosive, target orientated sport and should be treated as such, whatever your standard and however you see your dreams and goals. Before you kick a ball do you relax? Before you return a serve in tennis do you feel loose and free of tension? No! You are ready for action. Your body is ready to get kick started and to react appropriately so that you can perform at your best. So why should golf be any different? Please relax and push your backside out as far as you can just like a peacock does during his mating ritual.

Dynamic Foundation

Now your spine angle should be as straight and stiff as a snooker cue. Does this feel natural to you? So why are you preparing your body in this way? This can only lead to problems down the road, not only for your golf but also for your body!

Golf is a sport that thrives on controlled, explosive power. If you want to play golf at your best your body should be ready, not relaxed. If you want to rise to the challenge you need to change the way you prepare your body for your performance.

You need to put a spring in your step and be light on your feet as if playing tennis or football, dynamically prepared with muscles ready to perform. If you want to hit the ball long and straight to reach your full potential then it is imperative that your body is positioned to allow you to do so.

The correct starting position before you swing the club is more natural than is often perceived. Stand up and imagine you are waiting for a ball to be thrown in your direction. Amazingly you automatically flex your knees and lean forward with your shoulders, preparing your body for the catch. Now look at your hips. They are naturally pushed back due to the combination of the downward movement as you flex your knees and at the same time from leaning forward from your shoulders.

Dynamic, ready for action position; waiting to catch a ball

Your body automatically gets itself into position to allow you to perform at your best. The combination of flex in the knees and leaning forward with the shoulders not only naturally pushes your hips back; it also ensures that you remain perfectly balanced and ready for action. You don't have to think too much about it, especially when the ball is in motion with your body prepared to react. The underlying reason is that our brains function better and more naturally when we are reacting to a ball, leading to a throw, catch, pass or shot rather than when we have to set off the chain of events in a dead ball sport such as snooker, golf or a penalty kick in football. You will learn more about this difference and how to maximise the benefits of reacting to your target later in the swing.

Let's take the bending and flexing of the knees one step further and have a closer look at this natural yet often over analysed occurrence which takes place as we prepare our body for action. The *drop*, as I like to call it, naturally places your body's centre of gravity, which is located at the bottom of your spine, in perfect harmonic balance with the centre of gravity of your swing, which is positioned at the base of your neck. The base of your neck is the axis and the point of rotation and balance for your upper body. As you begin to build your swing you will learn the important role this plays by obeying some simple yet highly effective laws of physics.

The *drop* is you flicking the switch into sports mode. When playing football, tennis or waiting to catch a ball, you naturally lean forward with your upper body as you bend/flex your knees, which in turn pushes your hips and your body's point of centre of gravity (the bottom of your spine) backwards. Your upper body naturally leans forward to compensate for the backward shift of this point. Your body and the fantastic piece of kit lodged between your ears does all of this for you. Automatically the *drop* positions the bottom of your spine perfectly in relation to the base of your neck so that your balance is optimised. Your spine angle is straight, as it should be, before your back is thrown into any physically demanding task.

This is where many an *expert* will begin to shout from the tree tops that a stiff and straight spine angle is the back bone of a great golf swing. Yes it plays a major role but manufacturing this position or movement without the understanding

Signature Golf Swing: Stop fighting with complicated swing mechanics!

that it is a natural occurrence as part of the *drop* often results in a pain in the neck and back for the guy holding the sharp end of the stick. The key ingredient of a solid posture and the creation of a naturally straight spine angle as you address a golf ball is the correct relationship between your body's point of centre of gravity (the bottom of your spine) and your swing's point of centre of gravity (the base of your neck). You will be pleased to know that the bending of your knees as you lean forward with your shoulders does all of this for you, so *drop* the useless dribble with a spine angle as stiff as a snooker cue.

If you lean too far forward or backward with your upper or lower body this changes the relationship between these two points, resulting in a loss of balance and something which is even more devastating, a change in your spine angle at address and throughout your swing. This type of imbalance requires many complicated and inconsistent swing compensations resulting in a substantial loss of distance and control. If either the point at the bottom of your spine or the point at the base of your neck don't work in harmony your back and therefore spine angle will arch or be forced out of line with the natural dynamics of your body. Fighting with or ignoring these simple laws of physics will guarantee a dramatic weakness in both body and golf swing. So, it's about time you threw away the straight jacket and *dropped* into your optimum position, the way that Mother Nature herself intended.

Drop into position and allow your hands and arms to hang freely from your body. Now do the same thing with a golf club in your hands. You are not only dynamic my friend but athletically ready to fire up your swing

At address the hands and arms naturally hang down freely from the body

Another often over complicated and over analysed factor which has a direct influence on the position of your spine angle is the length of the golf club that you have in your hands. A driver has a long shaft which naturally produces a marginally upright posture at address in comparison to your posture at address with a seven iron. The shaft length of your seven iron is significantly shorter than that of your driver so therefore automatically your posture appears naturally more leaned over. This has absolutely nothing to do with the way that you address the ball but simply the angle and length of the golf club shaft running from the ground up to your hands.

Posture at address with a Driver   Posture at address with a seven iron

In simple terms the longer the shaft the flatter the angle and the shorter the shaft the steeper the angle therefore, when you play a shot with a driver, your posture will *appear* slightly more upright than when you are using your seven iron. Don't think about it, just do it! You are man not a machine, if you begin to play golf by numbers as many try to, the downward spiral of devastation will tear through your game leaving one beat up owner of a golf swing you will never trust in a month of Sundays. You will know yourself what feels balanced and ready for action. Let's have a look at where it all starts to go wrong.

Rock and roll

If, from here, you lean further forward with your upper body, your body weight naturally moves onto your toes. Automatically your point of centre of gravity for your swing (the base of your neck) is forced too far forward over the ball in relation to the point of centre of gravity of your body (the bottom of your spine). This will eventually result in a loss of balance and you falling flat on your face.

Your centre of gravity for your swing is now positioned too far forward and is no longer working in harmony with the centre of gravity for your body (bottom of spine). Your golf swing will have to be jam packed full of compensations to balance out the small physical discrepancies yet massive consequences that addressing your ball this way entails

If you now do the opposite and lean back with your upper body you will find that your hips are forced forward under your body to compensate and balance your body. The more you lean back the more your weight moves gradually onto the heels of your feet, eventually resulting in a loss of balance and you falling backwards. Your centre of gravity is now once again out of balance as your hips move too far under your body forcing the centre of gravity of your swing (base of your neck) too far back off the ball. The harmonic balance between the point of centre of gravity of your body (bottom of your spine) and the point of centre of gravity of your swing (base of your neck) is lost in a fight for balance. This scenario is setting you up for fairways full of inconsistent and weak golf shots that will hurt badly more often than you would care to admit!

Leaning too far off the ball at address forcing the body weight back onto the heels

Leaning too far over the ball at address forcing the body weight onto the toes

We have now covered the two major difficulties that golfers have with their posture, so let's see how this can affect your golf swing. If your upper body is too far over the ball or, as described above, you are leaning too far forward; your body weight will favour your toes at your address position.

During your swing this imbalance will need to be compensated for at some stage, usually with your body trying to find its natural centre of gravity. This results in your body often over compensating for your mistake at address, rocking you back onto your heels during your backswing. You are now at the top of your backswing with your body weight placed firmly on your heels which has lifted your body up and back out of its natural spine angle set at address to try to correct your balance.

You now have to throw another compensation in somewhere in your downswing, fingers crossed and you'll hit a good shot and average a steady one in ten.

If you begin your address position with your body weight on your heels a similar but opposite chain of events will develop in your swing, normally as you start your downswing, rolling you onto your toes.

Signature Golf Swing: Stop fighting with complicated swing mechanics!

If you find your natural centre of gravity as I have shown you, you can eliminate a wide range of swing faults. Your swing will be well balanced allowing you to start hitting consistently powerful golf shots. No two postures look identical as we are all built differently, with longer arms or shorter legs, but the fundamentals are always the same.

The rolling of body weight onto the heels as compensation in the backswing

Please follow these five steps and never forget your centre of gravity as you *drop* into your sports mode, dynamically ready to swing into action:

1. Stand tall with your back and legs in an upright position and your feet just inside shoulder width apart. Your body weight should be evenly balanced on both feet.

2. Extend your arms out in front of you at waist height with your club shaft parallel to the ground and grip in the one o'clock position.

Dynamic Foundation

3. The *Drop*: Lean forward with your shoulders and at the same time bend your knees.

4. Lower your hands and arms until your club head touches the ground. Let your arms hang down freely from your body. You have found your natural hand position.

5. Your hands should be slightly ahead of your correct ball position which is the next important aspect of your address position! Your left arm will now be an extension of your golf club with the blade of your golf club placed directly behind your ball, correctly aligned to your target.

To have a truly dynamic, ready posture position it is essential that your centre of gravity for both body and swing are positioned correctly and are balanced in total harmony. I have now described a great routine that you can repeat before each and every shot that you play; therefore you'll be safe in the knowledge that your body is correctly positioned. Be dynamic, get yourself ready and listen to your body. Golf is no different to any other athletic, explosive, target orientated sport and above all, remember never to fight with Mother Nature. You are the way that you are, your arms or legs will not become longer or shorter overnight even if you hang from the tree tops until dawn. Let your body find its natural position.

A question that I am often presented with is, "should my right shoulder be lower than my left at address?" Your body will get itself into the correct position naturally if you follow my instructions, you can rest assured. If you put your golf under the microscope then your game will become an oasis of angles and degrees that should really be of no concern and happen automatically. Little knowledge backed up with over-analysis is the best way to rock your golfing world, shaking it from the roots until it falls apart. In your grip your right hand is lower than your left which, in turn, realigns your shoulders and your right shoulder will naturally drop slightly lower than your left at address. As you build your golf swing with me shortly, you will find that many of the things that golfers constantly fight with happen automatically and are part of your natural make-up. You will also start to understand that a golf swing is a natural movement and many of the over-analysed technicalities happen within the motion. Don't give your right shoulder a second thought again at address, this is not something that you should be focusing upon, your shoulders (along with the rest of your body) will naturally fall into place.

Signature Golf Swing: Stop fighting with complicated swing mechanics!

Please don't over bend your knees, you should only flex them. Too much bend will push your hips out of position and create an arched spine. This is the best and fastest way to become known as the injury prone golfer who has to cry off every other weekend with a bad back.

Please don't think too much about your hand position at address. Let your hands hang down from your body naturally. There will always be space for your hands as your hips will leave clearance. Don't think in numbers, e.g. hands two or three inches from the left leg. A good guide is that your hands should be in a position below your chin, but this is also not one hundred percent reliable, just let it happen naturally.

Over bending the knees at address forces the hips out, creating an arched spine

At address the hands and arms naturally hang down freely from the body

Please don't favour your heels or toes with your body weight, this will only lead to problems in your swing as your body weight moves around to compensate. If your centre of gravity is positioned correctly your body weight will be spread evenly, producing a solid base from which you can build your swing

The body weight favouring the heels

The body weight favouring the toes

As you can see we have now set the stage for your swing, let your body find its natural position. After personally trying numerous methods of finding a good posture, I recommend the steps as outlined above. This method has proven to be the best, easiest and most consistent, that players of all shapes and sizes can use to find a dynamic, ready position that allows your body to move freely during your golf swing.

Please find your own individual, correct posture and never fight with the way that you were made. Find you own natural centre of gravity and your golf will thank you for it!

Check 4: Drop to be dynamically centred

To trust your golf, place it into the hands of a PGA Professional

Dynamic Foundation

Ball position: Play the easy ball

The ball position is often used as the easy way out for a majority of amateur golfers. What do you "Slicers" and "Toppers" do? As you turn a blind eye to your dark side, as golfers often do, your ball position gradually creeps further and further back in your stance until it has nowhere else to go other than outside of your right foot. You can't blame the ball or where it's sitting for your grass cutting worm killers or for taking divots that would fill a bunker.

I am taking you through the process of how to build your swing from the ground up with strong foundations and most importantly the easiest, most natural way for you personally to go it alone. If you are one of those golfers who moves the ball position around further forward or further back to make the most of a bad job then stop reading now and keep digging a hole for your golf career to topple into.

I am telling you this for your own good. One fault alone will set off a chain reaction of events that will turn a blue sky and lush green fairways into a boxing ring. After eighteen holes you'll feel as though you've just done ten rounds with Mike Tyson at his peak. A golf swing full of faults can be dangerous, so if you are one of those who is compensating by manipulating your ball position either pack it in or get used to the resulting aches and pains that crush your golf.

If you follow each and every point to a tee as I set your body up for your swing you will, I'm sure, surprise yourself. It may feel strange but I know it works. I know that you like having your ball position outside of your right or left foot and I know that this gives you a good feeling, but you are just tying yourself up in knots that will eventually strangle the life out of your golf. An incorrect ball position will make you look like the guy that is a million miles away from having his finger on the pulse.

Ball position too far forward/back in your stance

As you can clearly see below your shoulders are now pointing too far to your left in an open position. The opposite is also clear to see as your shoulders are placed in a position too far to your right, referred to as being closed.

Ball position too far forward   Ball position too far back

A poor ball position can wreck a great golf swing so imagine what it can do to the average amateur. There are no excuses for being lazy and neglecting a simple fundamental element in striving to be dynamic and ready to swing into action. If you do your golf will be erratic and at times very disappointing, you have been warned.

So if you want to improve your ball striking you need to establish a reliable, repeatable ball position. If you have played golf for a while you will probably be aware of the two different styles of ball positioning.

The Variable Ball Position

The Variable Ball Position is a method that moves the ball position through the stance depending on your choice of shot or the club that you have selected. If we begin using this ball position with your driver the ball would be in the standard position a couple of inches inside of your left heel. Now if you were to select a five iron your ball position would be approximately just left of centre. That's correct, I said "approximately" and that's why I don't believe that a Variable Ball Position can be accurate enough to offer consistently struck golf shots. As I have already explained your ball position changes your body alignment and if you are constantly moving your ball position around this just complicates matters. If I asked you again to show me where you position your ball with a five iron it's highly likely that it wouldn't be the same as the previous position. Now throw a little tournament pressure or some poor weather conditions into the equation and the foundations are starting to wobble. The betting man that I am wouldn't put any money on this horse.

The Variable Ball Position with a Driver and 5 iron

A Variable Ball Position has its moments, in special circumstances that require a shot that needs a little more imagination, but I don't believe it to be reliable enough to be part of your standard game.

Play The Easy Ball: The fixed ball position

The best way to propel your golf forward is to keep it simple and that's exactly what The Fixed Ball Position does. As its name describes the ball is fixed and doesn't move; this is the easy ball. For every golf club that you use and for every shot that you play your ball position stays the same, a couple of inches inside of your left heel. The major benefit is that you can always count on your ball position being the same, resulting in more solid and consistent golf swings (and shots) regardless of the playing conditions.

When you have your driver in your hands you know it's longer, you know it's more difficult to control and you can feel it demands more from you to support it. The basic rule of thumb is that the longer the golf club, the wider the stance needed to support the greater swing arc it produces. Very importantly the ball position stays the same, simple!

The optical illusion

The ball position stays the same, so why does it look further forward the longer the golf club and further back the shorter the golf club that I select? Your ball position remains fixed, inside of your left heel, for every club that you select. The optical illusion is created because your stance widens, making your ball position look further forward than it actually is.

Play the easy ball like this:

- When you are playing a shot with your **driver,** the ball position is two inches inside of your left heel. Your stance is no wider than shoulder width apart.
- When you are playing a shot with your **5 iron**, the ball position is two inches inside of your left heel. Your stance is slightly inside shoulder width apart.
- When you are playing a shot with your **pitching wedge**, the ball position is two inches inside of your left heel. Your feet are now positioned quite narrowly apart.

To keep it simple for crisp, clean golf shots every time, play the easy ball!

In your address position it is important to emphasise that your hands should be slightly ahead of your ball. Your left arm will now be an extension of your golf club which sets the correct angles relating to your hands, arms and body, ready for your backswing.

Dynamic Foundation

Driver   5 iron   Pitching Wedge

Check 5: Fix Your Easy Ball

To trust your golf, place it into the hands of a PGA Professional

Stance: Stand to deliver

Your ball position is now correct in relation to your stance.

So why are we talking about stance again? Your stance is how you connect yourself with the ground and how you balance your body whilst standing or moving around. The stance is something that most golfers overlook when playing a golf shot. In general, an average golfer's mind is full of technical swing information, grip and posture although it's not very often they have a good look at their stance. I can't emphasise how important your stance is, a poor stance can kill a golf swing stone dead.

It is often perceived that a wide stance offers so many benefits to your golf swing ranging from power to great stability. I am not saying that this isn't all true, it does offer a well-balanced strong base but were does it all start to go wrong?

Stance danger zone

If your stance is too wide, as is often the case with many golfers, this sets off a chain reaction of events that runs through your whole swing. If your stance is too wide and by too wide I mean any more than shoulder width apart, you will not be able to rotate your body efficiently in your swing with any of the weapons in your bag. Effectively your body will be blocked, which is not only bad for your golf but even more importantly you'll be forcing your body into places it really doesn't want to be.

If you stand facing a mirror and position your feet outside of shoulder width apart, you will now clearly see that this places your lower body in the most stable form, wide to narrow, a triangle. It is true that this offers great stability but lacks terribly in agility. Your body will not be allowed to move as it should and you must compensate during your swing in some way to allow for this simple fault in your address position. The most common form of compensation is the saddle-sore cowboy syndrome where you are forced to sway from side to side to avoid the pain. Your golf swing will look a little more than just tipsy.

After standing with a wide stance, even after a very short time, you will start to feel how this can be bad for your body. If you gently turn or move your body you will start to feel the pressure building up in your hips and lower back. Can you imagine the stress that this would place on these joints if you were to now introduce your golf swing? This has your **Golf Swing Danger Zone** written all over it.

Signature Golf Swing: Stop fighting with complicated swing mechanics!

Standing with a wide stance   Turning to the right and left with a wide stance

As you start your swing with your overly wide stance you will feel how difficult it is to transfer your body weight across onto your right side in your backswing. This causes your hips to slide across onto your right side and your upper body to turn out of sequence over to your left side, pulling your spine angle out of its natural position. Your left knee collapses, your left shoulder dips and your head loses height. This is the easiest way to produce one of the most destructive swing faults that there is in golf, the reverse pivot. A reverse pivot is not only detrimental to your golf but is a sure fire way to injury, particularly in the lower back region but generally anywhere from your head down to your toes.

A backswing with a wide stance eventually finishing pivoting over the left leg

Your natural weight lines

To get your stance into the correct zone is to simply stay within your body's natural weight lines. These run from the inside of your left heel through your left shoulder and from the inside of your right heel through your right shoulder. If you now face the mirror again and try to stand on your natural weight lines you will notice that your body runs straight from the ground up. Your body creates these angles naturally. If you stand as if you are waiting for a serve in tennis or a pass in football, you will notice the same similarities. Your body is now primed for action, naturally formed and ready to move as it should be.

Please don't fight with your body or place it in positions that it doesn't like, your body will hate you for it and so will your golf. It's about time you started to make life easier for yourself on the fairways. Imagine waiting for a bus, you wouldn't be doing the splits to spread your weight in an attempt to balance better unless you were just plain showing off on a windy day. You were made to stand within your centre of gravity on your weight lines. Trying to defy logic is enough to send your head into a spin, especially once you have a club, ball, flag, fairway and water hazard in the equation, not to mention those occasions when you have a shilling on the game as well!

The body's natural weight lines run from inside of the right heel through the right shoulder and from the inside of the left heel through the left shoulder

Strength comes from a well-balanced, athletic starting position, which allows your body to release its maximum power. In most sports agility is the key to great performance. On the other hand if your stance is too narrow it will knock you off balance which results in weak and inconsistent golf shots.

From my experience a slightly narrower stance will help your body movements to flow and work together but it is a fine line that you will have to get your own feeling for. Please follow the stance guidelines that I gave you earlier in "Play the Easy Ball".

If you want to play your best golf, please don't fight with the rules of Mother Nature. Find your individual natural position; this is the fastest and safest way to success on your fairways to heaven.

A wide stance will kill your swing. Stay within your natural weight lines and feel the positive effect that will run right through your game!!

Check 6: Stand on Your Weight Lines

To trust your golf, place it into the hands of a PGA Professional

Stand to attention

Align the clubface and your body correctly in relation to your target, ensuring that your ball position is correct for every shot.

This is a great method before you fire up your swing to ensure that your clubface and body are both correctly aligned, it also ensures that the ball is positioned correctly in your stance. This should be part of every shot that you play and is an essential ingredient in your pre-shot routine, covered in greater detail once you have built your swing. The pre-shot routine is designed to get your body and mind focused on your target.

Signature Golf Swing: Stop fighting with complicated swing mechanics!

Stand to attention and demand precision

1. Find a point within a metre of your ball, in line with your ball and the target line. Align your clubface to this point. Your clubface is now aligned correctly to the ball to target line.
2. Stand in the correct address position with your feet together
3. The ball is positioned in the middle of the stance

4. Place your left foot one third of the intended width of stance parallel to the ball to target line
5. Place your right foot two thirds of the intended width of stance parallel to the ball to target line.
6. You will now be standing in a square position in relation to your target.

Your clubface is now perfectly aligned to your target. Your feet, knees, hips and shoulders are now aligned correctly, parallel to your ball to target line.

You are now standing to attention: En Guarde!

To trust your golf, place it into the hands of a PGA Professional

Signature Swing

Every golf swing is like a signature!

To build a swing within the framework of your body, you have to realise that there are no two golf swings the same. We are all built differently, born with different styles and we all see the world through a different pair of eyes, so why would we all want to have the same golf swing? This is where many a man has slipped on someone else's banana skin in the belief that the new kid on the block has a faster bike and dips his head lower as he takes the corners, to win the hearts of all the girls. Simple you think, get your Dad to buy you a better bike and dip your head more into the corners but you'll soon find that trying to be someone you're not won't get you the girl because nobody likes a fake. Trying to imitate someone else's style by totally ignoring your own instinctive feelings is the fastest way to crash and burn in a mess that you'll never trust again. To really get the most out of yourself you have to find your own personal **Signature Swing** and build it from the ground up with your own system and your own two hands.

Over the years golf has produced some fantastically talented people who have also propelled the sport to where it is today. Each of these exceptional people has been individual in almost every way with the exception of their passion to win and desire to better themselves. Cheating was never in their vocabulary because as we all know a golf swing never lies. Great people in any walk of life know that you have got to do the most with what you have been given and focus on what you are good at and perfect it to rise above the rest.

In most cases, these same individuals are *technically* poles apart when it comes to the beautiful game of golf, due to the way that their bodies were made. However, a great golfer oozes charisma, feeling, rhythm, timing and a tremendous touch not only in practice but when it matters most. If you are running from the lions and are looking down thinking about how your legs should co-ordinate the movement you will be eaten alive before your knees even have chance to knock. The same can be said for any movement; golf is no different, so give it the respect it deserves. Your golf will love you for it. This will become clearer later when you relate golf to other explosive, target orientated sports. Fight with yourself on the fairways and all of the ingredients that go into making a great player great will vanish in a flash before your very own eyes.

The golfing legends of the past didn't have a manual full of technical advice to guide them or to refer to. They learnt in the fields or on the beach, with a stick and a ball, from instinct, feel, rhythm and timing, through the love of the beautiful game of golf. The golf that they played and the way that today's modern game is played is instinctive. I am a great believer that the game of golf should be taught from the grass roots up in a way that encourages a player to use his own natural ability with the fantastic computer inside his head firing on all cylinders, in the way that it was made to do. Next time you watch a big tournament and you see a player hitting a crucial shot to the final green, can you imagine that his thought process is focused on his arm, shoulders or hips? Maybe the only thing going through his head is something crazy like his target? No, it couldn't be, surely that's not the golf we know and love? It could never be as straight forward as throwing or catching a ball, could it?

Nobody showed the golfing greats of yesteryear how to shape shots, fade, draw, hook, slice, or how to fire the ball over or under a tree. They stood there for as long as it took to develop their technique from feeling, visualising the shots that they wanted to play. The game of golf that they played didn't come from a book, it wasn't man made. **The ball was their teacher and their target was the only thing.**

From my own observations the great players of yesteryear had great golf swings and they didn't study their every move because they didn't have the opportunity to do a split screen video swing analysis. Does technical analysis really deserve the credit it gets or can it be over powering? Video yourself catching a ball. Analyse the exact movements individually, take them to pieces and put them all together again. Now that you know how your perfect catch works then please be my guest and try to catch a ball whilst thinking about all this.

Do you really believe that Tiger Woods, the best golfer of his generation, "the legend, the master of the modern game", acquired his skills through over-analysis and only applying technical detail? Or did he begin his journey, as many other golfing greats do, as a child developing instinct and feeling firstly for the basics and for his target?

You could argue that golf has changed dramatically from this early era to the great stage that golf is played on today. An elite golfer is now an athlete with a total package from physical to mental excellence. Not only has the game become more professional but the equipment used today is not comparable even with the technology of ten years ago.

Signature Golf Swing: Stop fighting with complicated swing mechanics!

Have the basic fundamentals of the game of golf really changed? In my opinion the way in which we play the game has been analysed so intensely that it is now technically very challenging for players of all standards. Golf is an explosive, target orientated sport, and this is something that you have to have in the forefront of your mind, if you want to get the best out of your game.

Once you have developed a feeling for the direction of your target, you gradually move into the explosive, powerful phase of the game as you build your swing. Your whole swing revolves around your target and you progress as your instincts and feelings give you the green light.

Your body should be dynamically ready and your technique is important. As in any physical task, if you bend down once too often to pick up a heavy box and don't do it right, you'll bust your back. It's no different in golf. If you focus on your target, once you have the basic fundamentals in place, then there is a natural chain reaction of events that work without over-analysis and without you having to think twice. Start with no target or with faults in the basics and this will run right through your swing, devastating everything in its path. Without a target there is nothing to learn!

You have to find your own swing and develop your own strengths as the great masters have always done. Don't get me wrong, you will have weaknesses as we all do. We are only human, but don't dwell on them as there is no point, it doesn't make sense. Stop trying to become someone that you are not.

The secret in doing anything well is to firstly do nothing until you know what you are doing, little knowledge is dangerous. Stop listening to all of the influential master minds and experts running around shouting from the tallest tree tops about what's wrong or what the new magic move or quick fix is. Instead, why not find what naturally works best for you by applying the correct basics and by developing the secret that great players have known for generations: The ball is the best teacher and the target is everything. Has golf really changed so much or do we still only have two arms, two legs, a club and a ball? Would Jack Nicklaus in his hay-day have been able to hit the ball as far and crisp as Tiger Woods using today's equipment, with his swing of yesteryear? I wouldn't like to bet against it...

Every great player has a different signature, but written with the same pen (the basic fundamentals!!)

To trust your golf, place it into the hands of a PGA Professional

Your ball is not alive

Your ball is dead, it doesn't listen to you when you tell it to fly further or go into the hole unless you play it as a dead ball should be with the respect that it deserves. Don't underestimate the power of this for one minute, learning to play a dead ball will change the way you play golf forever.

A dead ball is often the reason you will see a top class footballer miss the target completely, ballooning the ball from the penalty spot. It's not only the long list of distractions such as the opposing fans or the goalkeeper that's the problem. Enemy number one, the devil in all of us, has time to come out and play, affecting the way we think and perform. This is the same reason you will see top class golfers miss two foot putts. If you have never thought of this before or were never told this before it's about time you got to grips with it, you have been served an injustice by your advisory panel.

You need to know that your brain automatically functions in a different mode when the ball is not moving. You need to practise and play in a different mode, which is a major part of any great player's game and pre-shot routine. When you compare most sports they are related in some way and very often the physical movements are similar, just adapted to the sport that is being played. Ultimately the ball will dictate how you play it and that is where the secret lies.

The science boffins are right on all accounts when it comes to playing a ball sport. When playing tennis or football this is something that you would normally never have to consider as the computer between your ears does it automatically for you, reacting spontaneously. Throw a spanner in the works by stopping the ball's motion and things start to look and feel completely different. This is the reason you can't quite put your finger on it but you knew golf was slightly different when relating it to your tennis or football career, whatever your level. This is the reason golf has the power and audacity to lift you up head and shoulders above your golfing buddies only to drag you back down again, more quickly than you can say boo to a goose.

This is the reason, my friends, that the golf swing has time to be analysed to death. It is pulled to bits and stuck back together again with imaginary sticky tape in a matter of minutes, all by numbers, as though it were a mathematical jigsaw puzzle. It is an understatement to say that this slows the learning process down. Push your nose to the screen and you start to see things that are not even there and I'm talking from experience here. I am not for one minute saying that your technique isn't important, it is in anything you attempt to do in life and a video camera in the right hands used to support your golf can be of great benefit. What I am saying here is that it is all about how you get there which is far more natural than many lead us to believe. In fact I myself have been stung by this one big time.

If you have ever wondered why your peers and you yourself my friend have made this game so complicated you have an excuse this time, you can blame the ball. This won't take your game to the dizzy heights that you dream about but might make you feel better. The easiest way around this one is to face it head on and learn to understand just how simple and effective playing a dead ball can be...

To trust your golf, place it in the hands of a PGA Professional

Play the dead ball

When your ball is not moving all of your natural instincts and feelings are taken away leaving you totally naked, with the fantastic piece of kit lodged between your ears working overtime, trying to figure the whole thing out. As part of the human race we are all judged on how quickly and effectively we can work things out and sound like we know what we are talking about. Often the danger is to over-do it and, as my great friend earlier once said, "Often something complicated is something simple that is just not fully understood." I am right with him on this one.

If your brain works best when it reacts naturally then you need to put your dead ball into the same scenario and play it using the same rules as you would play a ball in motion. This is where the most important influence on your golf game comes into its own, your target is not just the king it will eventually become the only thing. You are probably scratching your head right now in total bewilderment trying to work this one out, it's much easier than most of you will have ever imagined.

If you can't react to your ball because it's sitting pretty looking up at you then you need to react to your target. As I have already covered, most of the rotations and angles that make a good solid golf swing are naturally produced if the basic fundamentals are firmly in place. Yours will be. I am going to hold your hand through the building process, so relax.

Let's keep it simple here and imagine you wanted to teach your child how to throw a ball at a target. You would firstly place a ball in his dominant hand, ensuring that he had a nice firm grip on the ball. You would then look for a challenging target not too far out of reach but also not too close to bore the socks off him. You would then show him the technique which he would firstly watch with great anticipation. He would then repeat the movement without releasing the ball, looking at his target until he's ready to stand up to the challenge. He would then step up, look at the target and try to hit it.

He would of course need practice to develop his feel for the distance and height. His technique would develop through imitation until he had mastered throwing a ball. The ball would show him when he was correct or not as you can only be lucky once in a while. He would ultimately learn by doing and **the ball would be his Best Teacher, but without a target he would have had nothing to learn.** You would not even mention his arm, shoulders or what he should be doing with his head. If you did you'd still be there now, with a kid who can't throw a ball.

Very rarely is a virgin golfer told the important role a target plays in their development and how a target can guide the learning process. You are going to learn this here with me. Golf is often taught as part of a scientific equation that doesn't always add up. Turn your shoulders ninety degrees, turn your hips forty-five degrees, stick your back side out with a straight left arm and then try to hit the ball, it doesn't matter where it goes at first. Wrong! Your target is your guide and you should build your whole game focused around it, reacting naturally, using every last drop of feeling that you can squeeze out of your body. This is how every golfer should begin, not in a mass produced vacuum of one size fits all, it just doesn't cut it. Your target will become your only thing, just as the golfing greats have known for generations. It's about time you stopped wasting precious time and energy on things that don't add up and started to release the natural prowess that lives in all of us, the way you were made to.

To trust your golf, place it into the hands of a PGA Professional

Signature Golf Swing: Stop fighting with complicated swing mechanics!

Develop instinctive feeling for your target

Before you even hold a golf club in your hands you have to become familiar with the things that great players do to get a clear understanding of how important the basic fundamentals are. By this I don't mean turn your shoulders like Tiger, unless you are on the same physical excellence health conditioning training programme that is tailored specifically to your body and your golf swing like Tiger is. I mean rather that you should watch the simple things that they do well and how they prepare for a shot, whether it be a chip, pitch or full shot. If you look closely enough, you will see that the majority of them have one very similar trait.

As a great player prepares for a shot he is firstly striving to feel the shot that he has in mind. The only way that you can do this is if you have a target, which in golf is a flag or a position on the fairway and you aim your practice swings towards it. He addresses his ball dynamically, ready to swing into action, has a few looks and then lets his swing go. If we rewind to the "has a few looks" part of his preparation, what do you think he is looking at and thinking about? Allow me to let you into the secret; he is thinking about his target and where he wants his ball to finish. He certainly is not thinking about a physical movement so close to the execution of his shot. One thing you won't see very often is a great player standing over his ball in his set up position for a long time between looking at his target and letting his swing instinctively go.

If you want to really learn how to play a dead ball you have to use your brain and the way you were made to the max. The brain, as the scientific boffins have already confirmed, performs better when it is reacting naturally. These are the conditions you are striving to achieve during the preparation shortly before your shot. If you relate this to a penalty kick in football, often too much time taken over the kick is a sure sign that indecision has had time to creep in. The natural, instinctive, predator like behaviour has been stripped from the player's technique. This is the moment the odds start to stack up in the goalkeeper's favour.

To prove how strong it can be to develop your own instinctive feeling for your target, I want you to try to throw something, a ball or a rolled up piece of paper, at a realistic target. The first method I want you to try is as follows:

- Focus on your target for ten seconds then throw your ball at your target.

You will see from this exercise that you have had plenty of time to think about hitting, missing or even what you are about to have for lunch. This leaves the door wide open for the little devil to walk in and perch happily on your shoulder, chirping away at your instinct and confidence.

- Now focus on your target. As soon as you have clearly focused let the ball go and throw it at your target with no hesitation. React and trust your instinct.

The first time you try this it will scare the pants off you but will probably bring back pleasant memories from other previous sporting triumphs achieved whilst you were in your Zone. Your Zone is a quiet place and the best way to recall it is when you have achieved something without actually remembering how you did it, it was instinctive. If you are still confused, have you ever driven your car to work and landed outside of the doorstep without recalling anything that took place along the way? Then this is you in your Zone. I will cover the Zone in greater detail later.

Reacting to your target hones into your natural, instinctive behaviour and takes away the negativity and technical side of the shot you want to play. This is child's play and that's the reason children learn to do something at a faster pace than adults, they don't think about it they just do it. World class athletes and sportsmen either do this without realising it, or they work hard on this aspect of their performance. The next time you watch a crucial and deciding moment in a sports game you will see how this separates the men from the boys and the winners from the losers. Indecision is a killer where sport is concerned. That's why you are about to develop a routine that you will practise as you build your **Signature Swing**, eventually immersing this into your Zone. You can then take this onto the golf course with you, eliminating indecision from your game. With practice you will be fully focused and your mind, with its tendency to wander, will be reined in until you have played your shot.

From this moment forward you will gradually introduce the following three steps into each and every shot that you play:

1. Focus on your target
2. Focus on your ball
3. React to your target (hit the ball)

 www.golfswingzone.com

   1. Focus on your target   2. Focus on your ball   3. React to your target (hit the ball)

The amount of time you spend performing these three steps is in your hands. One word of warning though; if you take too long dithering over this you are leaving the door wide open to indecision. On the other hand, if you fly through these steps without true focus, your golf will become a blur. Thankfully we are all individual and you are no different. With a little elbow grease you will find a rhythm that suits your speed of play. Without the integration of these three steps your **Signature Swing** (that we are about to build up) will belong to nobody in particular, either that or it will be governed by your own little devils enjoying a free reign, as many a swing is!

On the other hand a **Signature Swing** built around focusing on your target and honing in on your natural instincts and feelings will propel your golf as far as you are willing to take it. Eventually you will be so wrapped up in your target that you won't remember how you got there.

This is one of the secrets the golfing greats have known for generations, enjoy my friend...

To trust your golf, place it into the hands of a PGA Professional

The Target

It is essential to understand that without a target there is nothing to learn. It really is as simple as that. Your objective is to get the ball into the hole in as few shots as possible, preferably in a few less than everyone else in the tournament or during a Wednesday evening with your mates. Yes we know all that, but how big should your target be?

Your target should be as small as possible, which really contradicts the guy who suggested you get your ball to within a bin lid (radius of one metre) of the hole on a ten metre putt. This guy does not understand how the brain works best and probably spends his life scratching his backside as he three putts from everywhere. A golden rule in any target orientated sport or task is: if you aim big, you miss big. On the contrary if you aim small, you miss small. This little gem will improve your golf more than you could ever imagine, so please don't underestimate the power of this statement.

Signature Golf Swing: Stop fighting with complicated swing mechanics!

If you wanted to hammer a nail into a piece of wood would you look at the whole nail? Amazing isn't it? Anything apart from golf is logical. You look at the head of the nail of course, the exact point that you want to hit with your hammer. You never once look at the hammer. A darts player doesn't just look at the whole board and never once looks at his dart; a footballer doesn't just look at the whole goal and never once looks at his foot. So why would you want to aim at a bin lid with your ten metre putt or at the whole fairway with your driver whilst checking to see where your elbow is or how your clubface is aligned during the stroke/swing?

Your target should be as small as possible and should be the main point of focus on each and every shot that you play. On the green the target is the hole or, if you are close to the hole, then pick a small area inside of it. When standing on the tee with a driver in your hands, a small branch or area of the fairway, or any prominent, distant land mark is ideal. It is often better to use a target that is off the ground as this reduces the risk of distractions and prevents those eyes of yours from wandering.

If the guy wearing those rose-tinted glasses steps into your space again with the bin lid tip tell him kindly to go run and jump into the nearest water hazard to look for his balls.

If you aim big, you miss big time, if you aim small you'll never be too far off the mark.

To trust your golf, place it into the hands of a PGA Professional

Signature Swing: 1st Gear

Signature Swing: From the ground up

This is where you begin your journey into a new world of golf. With the ammunition that I am about to arm you with you will build your personal **Signature Swing** from the ground up with your own two hands. I am not promoting any quick fixes here or easy ways out but I do know it's simple and easy to follow if you practise each step one at a time. The best bit is that you can do this on your own and you don't need someone constantly chirping away, firing running commentary at you over your shoulder.

Please make sure that you clearly understand every element of your address to get your body dynamically ready to spring into action. If you haven't followed my instructions you are wasting everybody's time and effort. If your grip is wrong or if your stance is all over the place you will build a **Signature Swing** that will gain you nothing, least of all your own respect. The only thing you will be guaranteed to gain is pain in your life! Please don't do anything until you know what you are doing with your address position.

You are now standing on the driving range

Use the guides that I am providing you with

Throughout my instruction I am providing you with controls that should form the backbone of your training. These are particularly crucial since I cannot be alongside you personally. They will be your guiding light, and all will become clear as we progress. They are there for a reason, not just to look good! If anyone questions the reasoning behind them kindly request that they keep their nose out during your precious practice time and go to www.golfswingzone.com

As I previously promised, you can do this on your own but you will need a helping hand to guide your swing. Your guides are your controls and safety net. Now is not the time to be lazy or sloppy and forget to bother with the guides, you are the one that will ultimately pay the price for a poor golf swing as your body soaks up all of the erratic, uncontrolled movements that you are programming into your bones. When your instincts and feelings give you the green light, then and only then dare you practise unaided. If you would prefer that your very helpful friend sat once again perched on your shoulder chirping away filling your head with a load of fairy tales, then be my guest. You will only be cheating yourself and believe it or not you will be cheating me a little as well, as it is important to me that your golf is transformed through my advice, since I know that it will be if you follow my guidelines. Why not give us both a big boost!

Select your target

Your target is the light at the end of your tunnel beckoning you closer and closer. Take your eye off it for one moment and you'll be left totally in the dark, dragging your heels, without a clue where you are heading. If you don't use a target for every shot that you play you are being a fool to yourself. Rather than golf you are playing pin the tail on the donkey's backside whilst blindfolded. Select a small target, focus on it and let it guide you as your ball teaches you just how much you are improving.

Club selection

Put your driver away for a while. Please don't try and hit it over the fence at the back of the driving range just yet, now is definitely not the time, leave the hero in you for later when you know what you are doing. Select a club that is easy to control and work your way through your bag as your confidence grows. The best way to destroy your first steps in building your **Signature Swing** is by thinking about distance. Start with a nine iron and stick with a nine iron until you have mastered the first part of your **Signature Swing** with it. Select a target that is easily reachable, even if it is only thirty meters away at the beginning, until you find your feet! You will know yourself when the time is right to start playing around with your club selection (and ego).

Tee your ball up

At the beginning you will need every advantage you can get. Trust me this has lots of benefits and really helps you to build your swing fault free. Do not see this as a cheat, having your ball on a tee at this stage promotes a free flowing swing and also encourages your body to stay in a neutral position. This takes away a little of the fear factor and stops you from thinking too much about topping the ball or hitting the ground. If you use a tee to build your **Signature Swing** I guarantee that you will have no fear of any position that you find yourself in on the course!

Guidelines

The guidelines that I am giving you here promote a consistent swing plane/direction that is then easily integrated into your full swing later, so please use them as I have described here.

- Inside of your ball, between your body and teed ball, place a golf club down parallel to your ball to target line. Do this with the club head at your target end, facing away from your body.
- Place a driving range basket or club head cover at the target end of this club; the club head will now cup the basket.
- Run another golf club from the grip end of the first club with the grip end of the second club again cupping the basket with the club head.
- Place a second basket opposite your right foot when addressing your ball, standing at shoulder width and one ball width outside of your teed ball.

This all looks much easier than it sounds as you can see here!

Guide ball or guide tee

You are standing on the driving range on your own so you need reassurance that you are on the right track as you begin your swing. If you follow these instructions you will have confidence in the fact that you are beginning your backswing on the correct swing path.

- Place a second ball ten inches behind your original ball and half a ball's width inside, which is in the direction of your body as if you had addressed your ball in play.

As you start your backswing away from your ball you should push the guide ball away from your target. This will help you to start your backswing on the correct swing path, leaving nothing to chance. This is also a great way to promote a good solid relationship between your hands, arms and body as they move away together early in your backswing. If you don't like the idea of placing a guide ball down for every shot you could use a tee on its own to replace your guide ball.

- Push this tee into the same position as referred to for the guide ball until only the head of the tee is showing. Use this tee as a reference point in the same way, beginning your swing off on the correct swing path.

Please don't focus on your guide ball or guide tee at any time during your swing. You should do this from feeling and instinct alone. If this is initially a problem for you then you should practise this without hitting your ball until you have found the correct feeling. Do not reach or over stretch for anything; allow your club head to come away from the ground when it is ready. Your hands and arms are only so long. You don't want to fall into the trap of **Swing Myth 5, "low and slow"** pulling your body out of position and moving totally out of sequence.

Signature Swing: 1st Gear

Guide ball

Guide tee

To trust your golf, place it into the hands of a PGA Professional

Signature Swing: Dynamic set up

- Grip your golf club correctly at the one o'clock position
- Place your club head behind your ball, aligned squarely to your target

- Your club is now an extension of your straight left wrist and left arm
- Place your feet together with your ball positioned just left of centre and align your body square to the golf club on the ground, parallel to your ball to target line

A quick reminder: I can't stress how important it is that your grip positions your left arm and left wrist as an extension of your golf club. It is fundamental to the control of your clubface that your grip places your hands in a position on your golf club that naturally squares your left wrist position parallel to your arm. If your wrist position is not parallel to your arm or your wrist breaks down during the early stages of your backswing then your clubface will flap around opening and closing all day long. If you overlook this simple golden rule your swing will never be consistent. I will explain the full significance when we start to build up to a full swing shortly in **Swing Myth 10: The biggest cock up**

The boss of any golf swing is the swing plane/direction. If your swing path is poorly directed you will be pulled around like a rag doll, bobbing and weaving yourself straight into your **Golf Swing Danger Zone** which is painfully ladled with inconsistency. When you place your feet together you *can't* run, hide or cheat by way of compensation in an attempt to manoeuvre your body around to straighten yourself out.

On the driving range with no pressure and the rhythm that comes from smashing ball after ball out there, you may be able to fool yourself for a short while, especially if you're the sporty type. As soon as you step on to the first tee with all that it throws at you, things start to look at little differently with a fake swing. You may feel as though you are King of the Range, but you will soon feel like a little fish in a very big pond when challenged by all of the predators waiting wide-mouthed for your first mistake on the open planes of a golf course.

The ball is your best teacher and it is here where your first lesson begins. When your feet are placed together and your swing direction is wrong it will be written all over your ball. Watch it, learn from it and then you can straighten yourself out. If your ball flight is too far left then swing more to the right to get back on track, it's as simple as that. When the boss is in good shape everything else will follow, especially when you introduce your body later. This is the reason that your swing direction must be your number one priority where your golf swing is concerned. If you want to build your swing on your own without the help of someone else then put your feet together. This is the most effective way to build your personal **Signature Swing**, with a solid foundation that you can really trust. Never forget that without a target there is nothing to learn!

In simple terms if your swing direction is incorrect your body will be blocked and forced out of position. This results in a substantial loss of power and leads to totally inconsistent golf. Perhaps this is no different to where you are right now? Until your swing direction is on line and you are instinctively firing at your target you can't even consider introducing your body. If you do as I suggest, with a little patience and some well rubbed in elbow grease you will truly have your finger on the pulse of your very own golf swing.

Improvement in anything in life requires controlled practice, and just for the record anyone who tries to convince you otherwise is lying through their teeth.

Aligning your feet, knees, hips and shoulders to the club on the ground, parallel to your ball to target line, is the safest way to be sure you are aligned correctly. Another big plus is that you will be practising standing well aligned to your ball which will pay dividends for you in the future.

Alive and Kicking: Posture dynamic and ready

A quick reminder: Flex your knees at the same time as bending forward with your shoulders. Be ready for action, not comfortable or wooden. Golf is an explosive, target orientated sport (I know that I keep mentioning this but I cannot express how important a point it is to realise!) You should give it the respect that your body deserves and treat it as one!

Please don't forget your centre of gravity for both body (base of your spine) and swing (base of your neck); this will be even more apparent and easier to feel now that you have your feet together.

Signature Swing: Mindset of greatness

You are now all set up and ready to get the show on the road. Just before you jump in head first, what were those three golden rules again that the golfing greats have known for generations?

- Focus on your target
- Focus on your ball
- React to your target (hit the ball)

I know your head is full with your dynamic set up and your guides are sitting pretty waiting for your **Signature Swing** to let rip but you must ensure that your whole swing building process is centred on developing your instinct for your target. This can only be achieved by focusing on the three key steps outlined above.

www.golfswingzone.com

Signature Swing: 1st Gear

In my mind the most important element of any golf swing is that your clubface is square in relation to the ball and the target throughout. Without aiming for a target, how can you ever be sure that your clubface is square? This is the reason I often point out that without a target there is nothing to learn. To gain an exceptional feeling for the control of your swing you will have to react to your target, squeezing every last drop of instinct out of your body. Instinctively reacting to your target will result in your swing eventually working on auto pilot the same way that you throw, kick or attack a moving ball. This is how your **Signature Swing** will be built until it naturally becomes second nature.

Focusing on the target at all times whilst feeling the shot required with free flowing practice swings; backswing target view

Focusing on the target at all times whilst feeling the shot required with free flowing practice swings; backswing side view

Focusing on the target at all times whilst feeling the shot required with free flowing practice swings; downswing target view

Signature Golf Swing: Stop fighting with complicated swing mechanics!

Focusing on the target at all times whilst feeling the shot required with free flowing practice swings; downswing side view

To acquire the feeling that you will need to work on auto pilot from feeling and instinct alone, you will have to programme your body to work in this way. This starts well before you hit your ball and is how a practice swing should be used. To help you to interpret your feeling for your target you have to immerse your practice swing into your target. The best way to do this is to focus on your target, remain focused only on your target and feel the shot that you are trying to play with free flowing practice swings. The golden rule of your practice swing is to never let your eyes wander. Remain sharply focused on your target at all times.

This is something that I will cover later in more depth in your Zone, and it is something that you will see top athletes becoming really passionate about just before a performance. Footballers score hundreds of goals in their minds before setting foot on the pitch, because they are so focused on their target. You will see elite athletes fully immersed, imitating the physical movement that their sport requires with only their target in mind. Your practice swing is no longer just a stretch or a warm up it is how you programme and prepare your body to react to your target. This is how your brain works best. A practice swing, when used correctly, will give your game the edge and your body and mind will know exactly what to do!

Your body is now prepared with the correct feeling that your swing needs to reproduce in order to hit your shot to your target. You are successfully programming your body. Step up to your ball, dynamically address your ball, focus on your target, focus on your ball and let your swing go. Trust it! You have to find your own speed of play that works best for you, allowing you to instinctively react to your target.

Every great golf swing is very similar in the first part of the swing, from the waist down. The reason for this is simple, the ball is sitting on the ground, and the first part of a consistent golf swing has to be solid and compact. Ambition is crucial, but running away with yourself will only cost you precious time and energy. **During the 1st Gear phase of your Signature Swing you are aiming for a half swing, no more than waist height.**

Your ultimate goal is a free flowing swing within your controls which is fully focused on your target. I will hold your hand step by step and will explain fully in clear detail how you should build your **Signature Swing**. Before we get started a quick *word of warning*, please do not break down each individual stage of your Signature Swing, free flowing and instinctive feeling is what you are striving to achieve here, you are a man not a machine.

To trust your golf, place it into the hands of a PGA Professional

Signature Swing: 1st Gear backswing

You are about to fire your **Signature Swing** into action like a breath of fresh air running through your game. Your golf is ready to be alive and kicking yourself all the way up to your **Top Gear**. You fully understand the value of your guides and controls. Your body is dynamically set up, raring to go. You are aware of the essential role that your target plays in the development and building process of your very own **Signature Swing**. Get ready to unleash your natural prowess and instincts, propelling your golf as far as you are willing to take it. It's in your hands...

Signature Swing: 1st Gear

A key fundamental during your **Signature Swing** building process is **the position of the centre line of your body,** which runs from top to toe and cuts your body in two, straight between the eyes. I don't want you to take this a step too far and start swinging like a wooden man, it is only meant as a guide. For some of you, maintaining your centre line will not be an issue, whereas others may initially struggle.

As in all sports good balance is a key fundamental ingredient directly related to your performance. Poor balance results in a substantial loss of power, control and consistency so it is rather important to the success of your **Signature Swing**. Your head should sit on top of your shoulders quietly as was intended, naturally balancing your body. Your body should remain neutral with the compliance of your hands and arms guiding it into position during your swing. Moving your head and body around in a struggle and fight for balance is a sure fire sign that something fundamental is out of whack. If this is you then go back to basics and once again prepare your body dynamically as I have taught you to and make sure that your controls are set correctly. Follow them!

In simple terms maintain a well centred body as you swing your golf club, this will help your body to stay neutral and will prevent your head from bobbing about like an apple in a bowl of water!

In **Posture: Alive and Kicking** achieving a dynamic and well balanced body in your golf swing is highly dependent upon the relationship between the centre of gravity of your body (the base of your spine) and the centre of gravity of your swing (the base of your neck). Throughout your **Signature Swing** it is essential that these two points of centre of gravity that were automatically set at address by the *drop* remain in harmonic balance. If at any given point during your swing their relationship changes then it will directly affect the positioning of your spine angle either lifting your upper body back and up out of the shot or forcing you to arch your back, both scenarios resulting in a blocked body rotation. The full significance and important role that this plays in the effectiveness of your **Signature Swing** will be fully explained soon on your way up to **Top Gear** in **Core Rotation**

The *drop* as in **Posture: Alive and kicking**. Flicking the switch into sports mode, preparing the body to be dynamically ready to spring into action

Correctly addressing the ball, dropping the body into position with the feet together ready for the 1st Gear: Backswing

www.golfswingzone.com

Signature Golf Swing: Stop fighting with complicated swing mechanics!

Take away

If you don't want to be dancing around every shot that you play in an attempt to compensate for a poorly aligned clubface then please make sure that you have **gripped your golf club from the one o'clock position,** as I have instructed. This places your left wrist and arm in a position which naturally runs down in line with your golf club. Your golf club shaft will appear as an extension of your left hand and arm

Please make sure that it is one of your main priorities to **hold a firm, straight left wrist position throughout your Signature Swing half backswing.** Strangling your golf club will be the premature death of your **Signature Swing.** Your goal is a solid left wrist as you smoothly move your club head away from your ball and into your backswing. You will feel for yourself the difference between firm and too firm, it's in your hands. Don't do anything until you know what you are doing with **Grip Pressure (Please don't release me or let me go!!) and The Golf Grip for Your Hands**.

The backswing smoothly begins with the main emphasis being on the maintenance of the firm, straight left wrist which was set at address

Please don't: cock your wrists, bend your wrists or do anything else with your wrists unless you want to spend time fighting with all of the clubface alignment issues that this throws in your face. If your **Signature Swing** starts wristy then you will be flicking, flashing an open and closed clubface at your ball all day long. I will go into detail covering how you should build your swing up from here with your wrists and introduce you to one of the most over-taught, biggest cock-ups ever to roam around golf club locker rooms later as you build your **Signature Swing** up to full.

A good tip that is often a big help is to maintain the triangle of your hands, arms and shoulders created naturally at your address position, throughout the first stage of your signature backswing. Not stiff or wooden, your goal is to be smooth and firmly relaxed. This encourages your left wrist to hold its position and promotes a one piece take away. This also promotes a swing that is well coordinated and that maintains the correct relationship with your body, consistently working in harmony with no disconnecting parts.

Guide ball/tee

As you move away from your ball push your guide ball away from your target.

Or;

As you move away swing over your guide tee.

The choice is yours but be sure to do it by way of feeling. Don't look at your guide ball or guide tee at any stage of your swing!!

Your objective is for your hands and arms to naturally swing around your body following the same path as you have now started them on with your guide ball/tee.

Signature Swing: 1st Gear

Pushing the guide ball away in the early backswing to ensure a correct swing path

Single Malt: Basket opposite your right foot

The first golf shot was played on Scottish turf six hundred years ago, so I believe it is only apt that you think of your basket as very expensive Scottish single malt. If you hit your bottle of single malt then your party is over before it's even begun.

Hitting the basket with a steeply disconnecting backswing; target view

Hitting the basket with a steeply disconnecting backswing; side view

Your bottle is your control, hitting it is a sure fire sign that your backswing is being started too far outside of plane, with your hands and arms disconnecting away from the natural rotation of your body. You don't need to know all of the ins and outs, just don't hit your bottle of whiskey unless you want to spend a small fortune on replacements. If your bottle is still standing after you have finished your practice session you have an excuse to celebrate your progress with a tot!

www.golfswingzone.com

Signature Golf Swing: Stop fighting with complicated swing mechanics!

After you have pushed your guide ball away or have swung over your guide tee your next port of call is to swing slightly inside of your bottle of whiskey. This will reassure you that your backswing is correctly aligned, guiding your swing safely on its way up to your half backswing position.

Correctly starting the backswing pushing the guide ball away

Please allow your hands and arms to *naturally* swing away from the ball, maintaining your straight left wrist and triangle at all times. Your hands and arms will lift up and away from the ground when they are naturally ready.

Please don't, as is often encouraged, reach in any way for the ground. Let your swing take its natural course. Your hands and arms were only made so long for a reason, don't try to over stretch yourself as you will pull your body out of position.

Into the goalkeeper's hands

Visualisation is a great tool to develop your golf with. A swing thought that will help you with your half backswing position and swing correction is to place your club head into the hands of the goalkeeper, wicket keeper or baseball catcher, whichever you can relate to best. Imagine one of these standing behind you in the crouched position, waiting for your club head at waist height. The goalkeeper's hands are directly in line with your point of centre of gravity for your swing which is positioned at the base of your neck. If you are unsure go back to **Posture: Alive and kicking**.

The goalkeeper's hands are at waist height directly in line with the base of the neck, the point of gravity for the swing

The *drop* is you flicking the switch into sports mode. When playing football, tennis or waiting to catch a ball, you naturally lean forward with your upper body as you bend/flex your knees, which in turn pushes your hips and your body's point of centre of gravity (the bottom of your spine) backwards. Your upper body naturally leans forward to compensate for the backward shift of this point. Your body and the fantastic piece of kit lodged between your ears does all of this for you. Automatically the *drop* positions the bottom of your spine perfectly in relation to the base of your neck so that your balance is optimised. Your spine angle is straight, as it should be, before your back is thrown into any physically demanding task.

Signature Swing: 1st Gear

For your **1st Gear backswing** to finish correctly as a well-balanced solid foundation on which to build your backswing and golf swing up to **Top Gear,** it is vital that you place your club head directly in line with the centre of gravity for your swing (the base of your neck). The centre of gravity for your swing runs from the base of your neck in a straight line down to the ground.

The club head correctly positioned at the half-way stage 1st gear: Backswing, resting safely in the goal-keeper's hands at waist height, directly in line with the base of the neck, the centre of gravity for the swing

This is the banana skin that many a golfer slips or has slipped up on at some stage in their career. If you miss the goalkeeper's hands positioned at waist height on the line of centre of gravity for your swing then you are prone to looping and jiving movements in an effort to regain your composure and control as you take your backswing to the top and beyond. This is first base if you like and this is a flashing red light; miss the goal keeper's hands and you will be scoring an own goal, big time! If you swing outside of the goalkeeper's hands then your hands and arms will disconnect too far away from your body limiting your natural rotation, forcing your body weight onto your toes.

If you swing too far inside of the goalkeeper's hands, yes you have guessed it, your hands and arms will swing back too close to your body, rotating your upper body too early and totally out of sequence. It will require a lot of bobbing, weaving and dancing around to compensate for this lot so don't even go there.

This is only meant as a guideline, it is not a problem if you are a centimetre or two too far inside or outside of the goalkeeper's hands. There is no need for you to stand there in front of the mirror trying to perfect this, use one by all means but never forget that meddling with over analysis is a dangerous game to play. If you follow my instruction and begin your backswing within your controls the way that I have explained, your club head will finish in the goalkeeper's hands without you having to think twice. This is merely a checkpoint to ensure that you do not stray too far off the mark. Feeling and instinct are the two main words in your golfing vocabulary so don't forget this by tying yourself up in knots with the technicalities of the swing mechanics; those days have gone my friend.

Finishing too far outside of the goal-keepers hands

Signature Golf Swing: Stop fighting with complicated swing mechanics!

Finishing too far inside of the goal-keeper's hands

This completes the half backswing position in the 1st Gear phase of your **Signature Swing.** You have allowed your body to naturally rotate gently, guided by the boss of your backswing; the direction that your hands and arms are swinging your club head in.

Clubface alignment

I know that I keep repeating the importance of maintaining a straight, firm left wrist throughout the early stages of your backswing but this tip is worth its weight in gold. For those of you that just don't get it or can't be bothered and want to overlook this fundamental rule, then read these words carefully…

If your left wrist breaks down by cocking or hinging in the early stages of your backswing then your golf swing is on a one way ticket to nowhere. The number one golf swing killer is trying every conceivable tip or trick to catch up with your poorly aligned clubface, leaving you dancing around looking like a dog chasing his tail. If I was to name the most vital element of a pure golf swing it would be how the angle of your clubface is aligned in relation to your ball and target. If you break this one simple golden rule you will be living in fear and will be the proud owner of a golf swing that you will never trust in a month of Sundays. You have been warned…

At your half backswing position you can check your clubface alignment in a mirror. Your club head should be sitting pretty safely in the goalkeeper's hands and your clubface should be turned slightly inwards at a position that would be showing five to the hour on a clock face. If you have gripped your golf club as I have shown you and your straight left wrist is in place throughout your backswing then all of these things will have happened automatically. If your clubface is one or two degrees out please take a deep breath, hold it and smack both cheeks with both hands at the same time reasonably firmly… If you are still looking for a degree here or there go for a cold shower, come back on to the driving range and walk straight past the mirror without a fidget or even a peak in sight, stop beating yourself up, your clubface alignment is fine.

If, on the other hand, your clubface is displaying some other slightly worrying signs then your left wrist has broken down in the early stages of your backswing.

If your **clubface is closed,** then your left wrist will have arched slightly. A reliable indication of this is when your hands move away from your body and your club head has moved too far inside of your hand position. Your clubface will be pointing too much in the direction of the ground.

If your **clubface is open** then your left wrist will be cupped slightly. A reliable indication of this is when your hands move too much in towards your body and your club head has moved outside of your hand position. Your clubface will be fanned open, pointing up to the sky.

Don't despair; we all fall off the band wagon from time to time. Take a few steps back and make sure that you are gripping your golf club correctly from the *one o'clock position* as I have described. Be sure to maintain your firm straight left wrist throughout the half backswing in your **Signature Swing**. If you follow me step by step you can do this totally alone. You will be pleased to know that you no longer have to listen to any of that poor advice out there, pushing and pulling your swing around like a rag doll.

Signature Swing: 1st Gear

| Correct clubface alignment | A *closed clubface* which points to the ground, too far inside of the hand position | An *open* clubface which points in the direction of the sky, too far outside of the hand position |

To trust your golf, place it into the hands of a PGA Professional

Signature Swing: 1st Gear downswing; Let down

Before you do anything please go back to **Swing Myth 1: Swing on the line of your target** and please don't do anything until you fully understand how a powerful golf swing works and what the boss of your golf swing is.

As I have already established, swinging back and forth on the line of your target produces a golf swing that lacks any power or consistency. If this is you and you are practising with this poor information in mind you may have already been drawn into an even worse scenario that causes you to swing to the left of your target. Without getting too technical if you have a backswing that is dominated by your hands and arms heading directly away from your target then you are prone to a backswing with little rotation. Your hands and arms will be flying high, disconnected too far away from your body due to the combination of your poorly directed backswing and the resulting lack of rotation. Your left knee collapses, your left shoulder drops, your head drops and your hips are forced across onto your right side. In the golfing world this is known as a *reverse pivot* and you are pivoting slap bang in the middle of your **Golf Swing Danger Zone** which is loaded with razor sharp teeth. I will introduce you to the **Golf Swing Danger Zone** a little later.

A steep backswing where the hands and arms disconnect away from the body. The left knee collapses, the left shoulder drops and the head drops, resulting in a reverse pivot over the left leg; target view

Signature Golf Swing: Stop fighting with complicated swing mechanics!

Side view of the resulting **reverse pivot**

From a steep, disconnected position too far away from your body in your backswing you have to make an almighty effort to get back to your ball by swinging back down towards your body. You are now heading to the left of your target, cutting across your ball and body with a ball flight that sticks out like a sore thumb, heading initially to the left of your target. If it's not your day you'll blow your back to bits and you'll be lying flat out on a hospital trolley nervously waiting for the results of your scan.

Downswing started outside of plane, swinging too far to the left of the target

Body weight forced onto right side due to body being blocked before, through and following impact, caused by a downswing direction too far to the left of the target; target view.

Signature Swing: 1st Gear

Body weight forced onto right side due to body being blocked before, through and following impact, caused by a downswing direction too far to the left of the target; side view.

If you are convinced that your ball flight is fairly straight and that you don't have a downswing directional problem, then just to be on the safe side:

- Select a target
- Address your ball and place a golf club down on the line of your feet
- Hit a shot

Body correctly aligned parallel to the ball to target line   Body incorrectly aligned to the right of the ball to target line

From the top of the backswing, swinging down back towards the target too far to the left in relation to the (poorly aligned) body at address

www.golfswingzone.com

Signature Golf Swing: Stop fighting with complicated swing mechanics!

Stand back after you have hit your shot and check how your body is aligned in relation to your target. If your body alignment is aiming to the right and not parallel to the ball to target line even if your ball flight is heading directly towards your target then you have been fooling yourself the whole time by compensating for your poor downswing direction with a poorly aligned body. You are aiming too far to the right of your target to compensate for your downswing path, swinging to the left.

The ball never lies; it is your best teacher, so don't argue with it, you'll come off second best every time!

Three great reasons to kick into touch the bad habit of a downswing that is swinging to the left (commonly known in the golf world as an outside to inside downswing path) of your target are:

A quick kiss goodbye

There is no love lost here, your club head doesn't hang around long it's just a quick kiss and goodbye. Swinging to the left of your target across your ball with your downswing cutting away off plane is difficult to do for any length of time, never mind for four hours or the time it takes you to complete eighteen holes. Normally the first few holes are fine until you fall into the black hole of what happened there? Then you come out of the other side shaken and stirred, to patch a little pride back onto your game for the last few holes.

The clubface cutting away from the ball before, through and following impact

Swinging to the left of your target cuts your club head across your ball. Your club head doesn't guide or follow your ball in any way, shape or form, it just glances across it which requires exceptional timing given to very few people. If you are one of those very few people then good luck with perfecting chopping your ball high and short into the air with every club in your bag. Even your driver will fly like a lob wedge.

Body block

Swing to the left of your target and you are placing your body into positions that not even a black belt could get you into. You are strangling the life out of your swing, chopping your body in two. Swinging to the left is totally blocking your downswing and follow-through, without knowing it you are standing in your own way all day long. By doing this you are losing a shocking forty to sixty percent of your power on average and are setting your bones up for a head on collision with your downswing.

This is the reason your driver doesn't work and the reason there is no difference in distance between your irons even if one flies higher or lower than the other. I nearly forgot to mention that your poorly directed downswing is the reason your neck, back, elbows, wrists, hips, shoulders, knees and ankles hurt like hell and the reason your physiotherapy bills are sky high. You will learn just how dangerous and painful all of this can be later in **Golf Swing Danger Zone**.

A downswing directed too far to the left of the target blocks the body and results in a substantial loss of power

Spray it all over

To top the whole thing off with a dollop of custard you won't be able to hit a cow's back side with a banjo. Your balls will fly, doing a loop-de-loop that the Red Arrows Elite Squadron would be proud of, up and down dale from one side of the course to the other. As a golden rule, swinging to the left of your target allows you access to a wide selection of shots suitable for every occasion, the only snag is you will never know which one is coming next. If you look on the positive side you will go places and see things that some golfers will never have the pleasure of. The only downside is it may cost you a small fortune in ammunition and may work out to be the hobby you can no longer afford. If you can't read between the lines what I'm trying to say is that swinging to the left of your target doesn't have a great deal going for it.

An outside to inside downswing path swinging too far to the left of the target resulting in a range of inconsistent and poorly struck golf shots

Set your **Signature Swing** controls and guides in place; if you are shattering your downswing single malt (which is to your left at address) into a hundred pieces with your downswing and follow-through, it's not just unfortunate it's a sure fire sign that your downswing is left, weak and miserably inconsistent.

Signature Golf Swing: Stop fighting with complicated swing mechanics!

Downswing sequence; swinging to the left of the target and smashing into the basket positioned to guide the downswing

To trust your golf, place it into the hands of a PGA Professional

Signature Swing: 1st Gear downswing; Angle of attack

Now we are getting down to the bare bones and to the raw framework that you will use to build your **Signature Swing** forward swing. The number one most important ingredient to go into the building process of a great golf swing, obviously once your body has been dynamically set up, is the direction of your golf swing in relation to your target.

As I have already established golf is an explosive, target orientated sport that thrives on power and precision. If you head for the slopes, straight to the peak where only the hardest of animals dare live and try to make your way steeply down through the deep powder snow without a well-directed swing with your skis, power and speed will be the last thing on your mind. If you don't believe me give it a try and you'll see for yourself as you lie there face down in the cold stuff and one rule of thumb; don't eat it if it's yellow. It's the same when you learn to ride a bike, drive a car, throw a ball or play tennis, the list is endless. Until you have the boss of your swing under control then and only then can you even consider packing the muscle on and beefing up your swing.

If your swing direction is out of whack your body will be totally blocked from naturally rotating, leaving you feeling sea sick with only a few shots under your belt. Your body will be pushed and pulled around like a rag doll. In this case your swing direction is not the boss of your swing but instead is the playground bully of your swing, beating you up every time you go to play.

We have already established that your swing path is your first port of call and you now understand that your downswing starts from a position behind your body, heading back towards your ball to target line. This appears as though your downswing direction is initially heading to the right of your target, recovering from your correctly rotated backswing until it hits your ball to target line, holding this line for as long as your body will allow.

Any explosive, target orientated sport uses your full body mass. The power of any physical movement uses the strength of your whole body, combining rotation and weight transference. This is guided to your target by the boss of your movement which is the direction in which you want to hit, punch, kick or throw.

Until you fully understand the last sentence do not do anything until you have once again read **Swing Myth 1: Swing on the line of your target.** You will be wasting your own precious time and energy if you don't fully appreciate the important role your swing direction plays in the development of your golf. You have been warned.

If you look at your controls and guides you will notice that one of your golf clubs lying on the ground is directed to the right of your target. Yes, you have guessed it; this is for your club head to follow in your downswing.

The controls, where one golf club points to the right of the target exclusively to guide the downswing direction

I also appreciate that you don't want to hit every shot to the right of your target, all will be revealed in just a moment. We have already established that a downswing direction that is swinging to the left of your target is weak and blocked. The same can be said for a downswing path that is swung excessively to the right of your target. I will explain this fully in **Golf Swing Danger Zone** later.

However a golf swing that produces a ball flight that is directed slightly to the right of your target is not just the bad shot of a good player, it is the bad shot of a great player. To the untrained eye it wouldn't be a bad shot at all because the ball would finish slightly more to the right of the fairway or green than was intended and the shot is typically well struck therefore loses no distance. This shot will never be too far off the mark.

You should firstly aspire to build your personal **Signature Swing** 1st gear downswing phase with a downswing correctly directed from behind your body. Your downswing path is now recovering from the position behind your body that was set by the correct direction and rotation of your backswing. Initially you have to swing to the right, back to your ball to target line and then continue on this path, swinging on the line of your target or slightly to the right of your target.

Correct backswing position at half swing **1st Gear: Backswing**

Signature Golf Swing: Stop fighting with complicated swing mechanics!

There are three main reasons for this approach:

Solid

Your club head will be guided by your swing direction and will remain with your ball before, through and following impact, for the maximum amount of time that your body and swing will allow. Your golf shots will be solid and very consistent. Under extreme circumstances such as poor weather conditions or tournament pressure you will be safe in the knowledge that your timing doesn't have to be one hundred percent. If you miss your sweet spot your ball will have the full height and breadth of your club head to take the hit, there will be no twisting or cutting away off plane; your bad shots will never be that bad again.

Precision

Only a fool would suggest that you will never hit a bad shot again when your **Signature Swing** is fully built. One thing I can say with confidence however is that your percentage success rate will go through the roof and you will be happy to live with your bad shots. Your pure swing path will work in harmony with your body. Your balance and centre of gravity throughout your swing will be faultless, unless you try something a little too extravagant, after all, there's a little devil in us all, no risk no fun. As your **Signature Swing** naturally develops it will choose a dominant, consistently shaped shot made to measure to fit you and your swing like a glove. This can be exceptionally effective when used in the right place at the right time; be patient, all will be revealed in due course.

Power

Your swing direction rules the roost when it comes to the pecking order of your golf swing. It is the boss of your swing and your body follows its lead. The direction that you swing your hands and arms in, when correct, automatically guides and rotates your body into position. This is no different to when you throw a ball, hit a tennis shot or when a boxer throws a knock-out blow; you never once think about how your body has rotated. Your body is free to turn and move as it was made to do so and you will reap the full benefit of your body mass in every phase of your swing. If your swing direction is correct in relation to your target you will be utilizing all of your major muscle groups to the max, bulking up your swing and unleashing your full potential. The sky is the limit...

Correct angle of attack before, through and following impact

To trust your golf, place it into the hands of a PGA Professional

Signature Swing: Downswing; Move through the gears

To build your own personal **Signature Swing** successfully from the grass roots up to full bloom requires controlled step by step military like precision. As you become familiar with your new found swing movements you can work through each step, gradually integrating them with instinct and feeling for your target until they become married as one. The three key ingredients (in order) are:

- **1st Gear: Swing direction**
- **2nd Gear: Clubface alignment**
- **3rd Gear: Body**

3rd Gear: Body with correct swing direction and clubface alignment

Your controls have now guided your backswing into position. Your straight and firm left wrist is your safety net ensuring that your clubface is squarely aligned throughout your half backswing position. Your 1st Gear backswing phase is complete; it's normally the forward swing that starts to cause the majority of the headaches. However you can be reassured that you have me, your controls and all of your guides in place; nothing is going to get in our way, I will make sure of it!

Your **Swing Direction,** as we have already established, is the boss of your swing. That's the reason, as you put your foot gently on the throttle, that this is your 1st Gear. The quality of your swing path ultimately decides how consistent and inevitably how good you will be. If your swing direction is out of whack then your clubface is either correctly aligned to it heading in the wrong direction or correctly aligned to the target and either open or closed in relation to your swing direction. It is pointless trying to firstly correct or maintain a clubface square to your ball and target in your downswing if the direction of your swing is heading somewhere else. I have already established that a left downswing is *weak* and a downswing too far to the right is also erratic, ladled with weaknesses of every size and shape imaginable. The main goal of the 1st Gear in building your **Signature Swing** is *a downswing direction where your ball initially begins its flight path slightly to the right of your target.*

For the feeling to be fully ingrained and programmed into your muscles will require some well rubbed in elbow grease. If anyone tells you any different they are either trying their hardest to sell you something or have never tried this for themselves. Firstly establishing a correct and pure swing direction is the best way to build a strong base for your swing and is a crucial part of the framework. As your swing feelings and instincts develop they will give you the green light to progress through the gears of your **Signature Swing.** Your **Clubface Alignment** is the next phase of the building up process as you move up to 2nd Gear. The main objective is to bring your swing direction and clubface alignment together, squarely firing at your target. Your goal is for a harmonious relationship eventually marrying your swing direction and clubface alignment with the release (rotation) of your hands in your downswing. With practice your downswing direction and clubface alignment will come together, firing instinctively at your target.

When your instinct is King of the Castle and your target, as the golfing greats have known for generations, is the only thought to cross your mind, then and only then can you put the cherry on top of the cake. Your **Body** is last but not least, moving you up to 3rd Gear. Why? If your swing direction and clubface alignment are heading in the wrong direction your body will be bullied, pushed and shoved from pillar to post every time you go out to play. Your body will be totally blocked from performing natural movements that are second nature to all of your hinging and moving joints, the movements that they were made for. It doesn't matter how long you stand on the driving range perfecting your rotation and weight transference, if your swing direction is wrong and your clubface is poorly aligned you will be the unfortunate owner of a weak, misfiring golf swing.

You will know yourself when the time is right to widen your stance and beef up your swing to pack on the muscle, it will be written all over your ball; never forget it's your best teacher. When your swing direction and clubface alignment are fully yours the introduction of the rest of your body will add a totally new dimension to the game of golf you love so much. Your ball flight will penetrate through any wind, hail, sleet or snow without even a hint of indecision. You will be left open mouthed by the improvement in your performance as we gradually progress together through the phases of your **Signature Swing**, eventually hitting your **Top Gear**.

The substantial improvement in the distance your ball carries and travels will take some getting used to as you overshoot greens and fairways with two or three clubs less than before. At first it may be frustrating coming to terms with your new found power and distance, but it's a similar problem that the guy who has just won the jackpot in the lottery has; at first he doesn't know what to do with it all until it hits home that he can now live the dream he thought would never come true. It's not difficult and it's not filling your head with a load of things that don't add up. It's simple, powerful and very effective. Have you ever wondered why great players swing easy and hit long? Look no further, it's not rocket science and it's totally within your grasp. Your golf is in now in safe hands, if you follow me to a tee I promise you won't believe your eyes...

To trust your golf, place it into the hands of a PGA Professional

Signature Swing: 1st Gear: Downswing direction

The first step on the way to building your **Signature Swing** from the ground up on solid foundations is the direction of your downswing.

Follow your guide

All of your guides and controls are in place. You are aiming for a ball flight that begins slightly to the right of your target. Your club head should follow the golf club within your controls which is pointing to the right of your target. This is to aid your swing direction. If your ball flight is heading too far to the right of your target then you have over-cooked it. From here you have to work back to your target to correct your swing direction.

The downswing guided by the club within the controls ensuring that the club head remains with the ball for the maximum duration

If your ball is spinning wildly left or right even though your grip is correct and your clubface is squarely aligned to your target at address this is not a priority in the 1st Gear stage of building your **Signature Swing**. Clubface alignment is your 2nd Gear phase during which the spin on your ball will be addressed and corrected accordingly. Your number one concern and the only thing you are interested in here as you start your downswing building process is the initial direction of your ball directly following impact. What it does from here will be simply ironed out in 2nd Gear, please don't run, skip or jump before you can even crawl.

Your goal is simple. All that I want you to do is try to hit your shots consistently five or ten metres straight to the right of your target. If needs be choose a second target to the right of your original target to guide your downswing and follow through. Follow your guide; it is there for a reason. You are building this swing with the two hands of the most important golfer in your world, you of course! It is therefore imperative that you practise in a controlled environment to be sure that you are programming your body with the correct information. I am not standing there with you holding your hand so you need to follow your guides and controls to keep you on the straight and narrow. If you do stray then work your way back, it is as simple as that.

The 2nd single malt: Basket

Time for another tot of the finest for your downswing and follow through. If you look to your left you will see your bottle of single malt looking straight back up at you. If you smash into this bottle with your club head in your follow through this is a sure fire sign that your downswing is still a little tipsy. Keep doing it and it will cost you a small fortune, not in whiskey but on the treatment table of your local physiotherapists (or worse still your back surgeon). All will be revealed later in **Golf Swing Danger Zone**.

Downswing direction swinging too far to the left of the target

If you decide to remove this bottle from your controls because you have smashed it too many times and can't be bothered replacing it for every shot then do me a favour and pick the lot up, *the time has come for us to part company*. If you are serious about the improvement and development of your golf then don't be surprised to learn that it might require some patience and trust on your part. Believe me this really works and you can build your swing from the ground up with your own two hands. The only condition is that you build your **Signature Swing** gradually at your own pace, within a controlled environment. Say no more, the choice is ultimately yours my friend.

A correct **1st Gear Backswing**, Downswing and Follow Through controlled by the guides

You should be and will be aware of the bottle in every stage of your downswing. It has been placed there for your benefit to do the job it's supposed to do, remove it at your peril. Each and every part of your guides and controls are there to help you physically and subconsciously program your body to draw the best from your game. Only when you are fully in control and your **Signature Swing** really belongs to you can you even consider continuing unaided! Learn to love your guides; they are saving you a fortune. Your practice time is productive and they will give you so much in return, a golfer's best friend. You will know better than me when you are ready to go it alone.

To trust your golf, place it into the hands of a PGA Professional

Signature Swing: 2nd Gear

Signature Swing: 2nd Gear: Clubface alignment

The release or the hand rotation before, through and following the impact position is a natural occurrence in the majority of explosive, target orientated sports that can be easily explained. Any sport that requires power directed at a target such as football, tennis, martial arts, golf or even when throwing a ball all use the power that is created within the body's weight transference and rotation around its core (centre of gravity). An explosive, target orientated sport is therefore based upon a rotational movement.

Golf, due to the nature of the sport using a dead ball that is static (and not in motion), is often severely over analysed, almost to breaking point. Within the golfing world the release (control of the clubface through the hitting area) in my mind is not always clearly explained to the man on the street holding the sharp end of the stick.

I will prove my method of how simple and natural the release is by once again using the example of throwing a ball, which I explained in detail in **Swing Myth 1: Swing on the line of your target.** Throwing a ball is a great example that all walks of life can relate to and which, as the majority of explosive target orientated sports do, inherits the same physical characteristics as a purely swung golf swing.

Please use **Swing Myth 1: Swing on the line of your target** for reference if needs be. You should now have a clear picture in your mind's eye of the direction of a correct golf swing in relation to its target and how the basic movements are formed, from the information that I have armed you with throughout the building process thus far.

- You are standing parallel to your ball to target line with your ball in your right hand which is directly in line with your target, no different to your address position in your golf swing.

- As you pull your ball back with your right hand around and behind your body your body weight transfers across to your right side within a natural rotation. Guess what? Your hand has also rotated with your body, eventually finishing with the palm of your right hand facing directly away from you. This is very similar to the top of your backswing.

Signature Golf Swing: Stop fighting with complicated swing mechanics!

- As you start back attacking your target with your ball hand, recovering from the position behind your body, the direction of your ball hand and the weight transference rotates your body back to your left side. Your ball hand also turns back in synchronisation with your body, very similar to the beginning of your downswing.

- As you approach releasing point the palm of your hand faces directly towards your target, maintaining this position as you release your ball and for a short time after release. This is very similar to your impact position and early follow-through.

- Eventually your natural rotation and body weight shift forces your right hand and arm past your target line to finish in a position around your body. The palm of your hand is now facing towards your body. This is very similar to the finish position of your golf swing.

This is probably something you have never given a second thought to when you are throwing a ball but golf however is a completely different animal with razor sharp teeth that don't want to let go of the complicated stuff. If it was easy then the jungle that golf lives in wouldn't have quite so many well looked after juicy, sweet bananas.

Signature Swing: 2nd Gear

The example of throwing a ball is no different to the examples that I could take from the majority of other explosive, target orientated sports or physical movements. I know it might not be a perfect match if you are a professional javelin thrower so fine, hammer me into the ground for drawing breath. As you can now appreciate it's not too far from the mark, apart from the run up, unless you would like to start a new golfing craze. Every sport has its own unique idiosyncrasies that are inherited by the sport in question, but the body uses its full capacity in each one with many similar comparable traits.

I strongly recommend that you don't allow anyone to fill your head with a load of mumbo jumbo that has the power to seduce and brainwash the vulnerable or the newbie's. Wearing coloured patches on gloves or prancing around with a beach ball rammed to your chest between your arms to see which triangle you finish on as you rotate will leave you acting and feeling like a clown. A poorly understood and executed technique will eventually catch up with you and bite you to the bone as you will find out later in **Golf Swing Danger Zone**.

The choice is yours, I've been there and done that and have been sold many a T-shirt full of props that the majority of pantomime donkeys would be proud of. My dad had to build a shed so that he could fit his car in the garage so don't fall into the same traps as me who naively squandered all of his paper-round money on a load of dead ducks.

Release your clubface alignment

If you have followed my instructions then your **Signature Swing** half backswing will have turned nicely around your body as it should. You will have maintained your square, firm left wrist which secures a square clubface position as your hands and arms have naturally rotated in unison around your body. You can rest assured that your clubface alignment is correct.

1st Gear: Backswing ensures that the clubface is squarely aligned

The golden rule for any good/great golfer is; the ball is your best teacher. Watch, listen and learn from every inch of feedback it throws back at you, it is priceless!!

When you throw a ball we have already established that the majority of you would not even contemplate how your hand turns during the throw. Normally this would not even enter your head unless your sport allowed you to take advantage of the situation, such as a bowler or pitcher in cricket or baseball, purposely catching the batsman unawares. Golf, at times, can also require drastic measures in special circumstances. Advanced players can capitalise on the amount of spin they put on their ball, to either get themselves out of jail with a well-shaped recovery shot or to maximise their control using spin, to stop their ball stone dead on the green. As soon as you have built your **Signature Swing** and have fully got to grips with it I will introduce you to the world of advanced shot making, made easy, as you'll soon find out.

We are starting with the basics here, as every great player does. In most walks of life if the basics are firmly in place then the rest is just fluff and flowers, sold well by the guy in the rose-tinted glasses. Eventually when you reach your **Top Gear** your **Signature Swing** will be fit for a king, no different to that of a top flight professional with, of course, the heavy influence from your side of your own personal goals, physical characteristics and your drive and determination to be the best. If you just want to have more fun and better your game and don't have the time and determination to be the next Tiger you will also be building your swing up the same way within your own physical, mental and realistic borders, smashing your all time bests into oblivion in the process.

Signature Golf Swing: Stop fighting with complicated swing mechanics!

Natural release

When you throw a ball you don't think about the release, your natural rotation and weight transference turn your hand naturally in the throw, in unison with your body. For many of you the release in your now correctly aligned downswing path will gradually integrate and marry together with your ball flight. Your ball flight now begins and continues its flight slightly to the right until your natural release intervenes by squaring it up to your target, a match made in heaven. If your swing direction is correctly aligned as I have instructed in **Signature Swing: 1st Gear; Downswing direction** this will encourage your hands and arms to rotate naturally within the movement, gelling the two gears together. As your **Signature Swing** direction develops so will your rotation and release, without too much effort or brain power. A golf swing is basically a rotation around a well-balanced core (body), firing at a target. By swinging within your guides and controls your hands will inevitably have to release at some stage during your downswing.

It's not always plain sailing, as some of you will also experience, especially if you have already played for some time and have naturally developed your own muscle memory for swing movements, often compensating with a poorly executed release in an effort to dance around your swing directional problem. You will discover later the power of muscle memory and how to maximise it to use it to your advantage in **3 Steps Correct**. Two wrongs don't make Einstein and will drag you straight into your **Golf Swing Danger Zone**. If it's not your day then be prepared, it's going to hurt like hell.

A word of warning. Your first port of call before you try to tackle your release correction, if it's not quite in synch with your swing path, is your dynamic set up, grip and grip pressure. Don't do anything until you know what you are doing in all of your basic set up stages or you will feel as though you have just got off a ride at the fairground, dizzy and totally disorientated. You will be wasting precious time and energy in search of an answer.

Under-active release

An under active release is when your hands are not rotating in unison with your body during your downswing, impact and follow through. This leaves the blade of your golf club open, producing slice spin, curving your ball to the right. It could simply be that your release is after impact which is far too late, having no effect on your ball flight as your ball is already on its way.

- Smoothly turn your right hand over your left

Your release begins in your downswing. The timing of your release is a matter of personal preference and is ultimately decided by your ball flight. This will guide you by showing you where you are going wrong. **A word of warning;** never try to release at your ball, if you do then nine times out of ten you will be too late or it will all finish in a mad, uncontrolled rush to square your clubface up in time to hit the ball. You will finish your swing looking like you are walking on a bed of nails, tip-toeing around trying to recover your balance just as good old Uncle Jack does in the middle of the dance floor at the end of every family wedding. Don't even go there!

Signature Swing: 2nd Gear

To rev up your release you should start by trying to introduce it as you begin your **Signature Swing** half-length downswing smoothly through impact and into your follow-through. Your ball is your best teacher and will hold your hand through the process. All you need to do to activate your release and square your clubface through impact is to smoothly turn your right hand over your left. Gradually build up the intensity of your release until your clubface alignment is working as one with your downswing direction, firing at your target. Be patient (which I know is easier said than done) and great things will happen. **A word of warning;** if your grip pressure is too strong your hands will be blocked from releasing. Your grip should be firm enough to maintain an even hold on your golf club handle. If your golf club grips are torn to shreds within a hand full of games and your glove only lasts two minutes you are gripping your golf club like a gorilla!

Over-active release

An over-active release is when your right hand turns over your left too early or too quickly out of sequence with your body, closing the blade and resulting in a ball flight that curves to the left. All of the same ground rules apply as with an under-active release but you should tackle this problem slightly differently as follows:

- Smoothly turn your right hand under your left

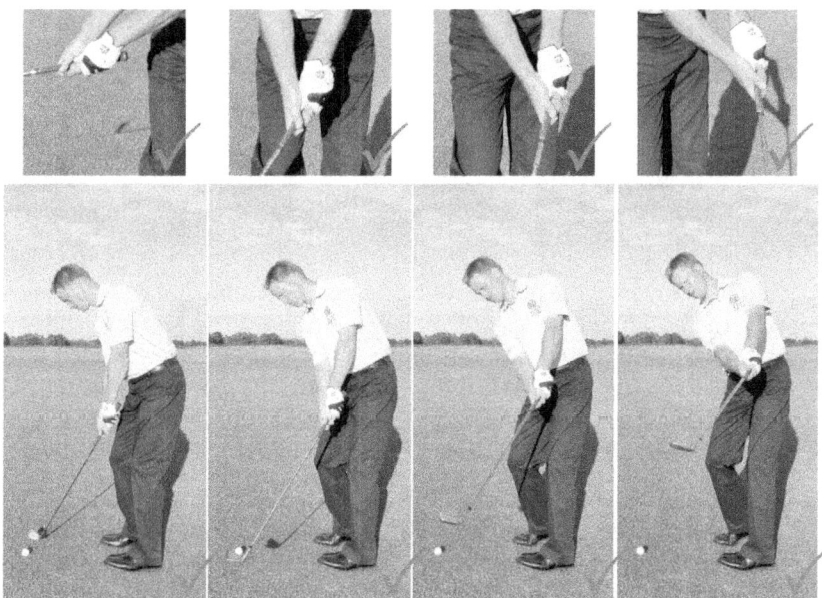

- Place slightly more grip pressure on the last three fingers of your left hand throughout your whole swing
- Hold the clubface square to your target at impact and into your follow through
- Hold the clubface as if pointing to the sky in your follow through

Golf is all about feeling, try all of the above and you will soon feel which one fits your hands best. Smoothly turning your right hand under your left is very effective for the majority of golfers when used to correct their over active release, the gold stamp if you like. Placing slightly more grip pressure on the last three fingers of your left hand restricts your hands from turning and over-releasing. If you have a problem with grip pressure this will be apparent within your first few shots as your grip slips on the handle of your golf club.

A clear indication of a poor distribution of grip pressure during your swing is the tell-tale hole that appears in the palm of your glove. Holding your clubface to your target or to the sky in your follow through are both designed to encourage your clubface to correct the over-active release of your hands by holding the release off. Using the feedback your ball throws back at you with one of the four or two of the four correction options listed above will bring your clubface alignment and swing direction together to work in harmony.

To trust your golf, place it into the hands of a PGA Professional

True impact

- Focus on your target
- Focus on your ball
- React to your target (hit the ball)

Not until you are firing your ball at your target with only your target in mind can you say that the 1st and 2nd Gears of your **Signature Swing** truly belong to you! If you want to make a big impact with your golf you have to work outside of your technical mode and be fully focused on your target-oriented mode of play. If you were swimming from the sharks in an attempt to get back to shore and were thinking how your hands and arms should move then you'd be nothing but a sitting duck way out of your depth.

Without a target you are lost. To really play the golf of your dreams is possible but one key ingredient must firstly be in place; the whole development and building process of your **Signature Swing** has to revolve around your target. Your ball is your best teacher but without a target there is nothing to learn, it really is as simple as that. Without a target you never truly know when you have hit a great shot or a terrible shot; you have no judge and are being a fool to yourself. If you have never been told this before or were not aware of the important role a target plays in your improvement or success then you had better get your head around it now!

Before you can beef up your swing and pack on the muscle by introducing your full body onto the scene you have to be instinctively reacting to your target, with your swing direction and release firmly glued together, working as one. It may take a little time, patience and elbow grease but it will be worth its weight in gold when you become the master of the boss of your swing. When your swing direction and release are fully honed onto your target the majority of your ground work has been completed. If you fall off the band wagon, as all great players do from time to time, then you are armed with the knowledge of how to get up, dust yourself down and build yourself back up to be stronger than ever before. Practising within a controlled environment with your target as your main point of focus will blow your mind.

I must point out that at this stage you are not striving for distance and power; if you tried to throw a ball with only your hand and arm how could you expect to cover much ground even if you had an arm like Popeye? Smooth, under control and instinctive is the way forward for your **Signature Swing** to truly make waves and have a real impact on your golf. There are no short cuts or quick fixes and easy ways out but the benefits of a little hard work and patience together with the correct technique will last a lifetime.

- If you throw a ball, how do you do it?
- If you kick a ball, how do you do it?
- If you catch a ball, how do you do it?

This is the secret my friends, the secret that great players have known for generations!

When your instincts have given you the green light then and only then can you move up through the gears, all the way up to your **Top Gear**.

To trust your golf, place it into the hands of a PGA Professional

 www.golfswingzone.com

Signature Swing: 1st and 2nd Gears; Step up to the challenge

As I have promised all along you can build your own **Signature Swing** from the ground up, with your own two hands and it will gradually evolve into a golf swing that fits your body like a glove. I have armed you with the ammunition that will fuel your progress. This is where you will come into your own, the butt stops here, and it's now in your hands. I will always be here to guide you, so before you jump in head first with the muscle and take your swing up to the dizzy heights of your 3rd Gear you will need to be sure that you have a tight reign over the boss of your swing.

It won't happen overnight and don't let anyone pull the wool over your eyes with promises like, "drop your handicap like a hot potato in one week". I have been in this business long enough and maybe I'm already too long in the tooth to listen to this kind of slippery sales pitch any longer. This is the sweetener to draw you in, trap you and make you throw your cash around like confetti.

Your golf will significantly improve gradually as you work through the building process within your controls and with your target to guide your success. I will be totally honest with you, the tooth fairy won't come down and sprinkle you over the head with magic dust and do the job for you. It will take practice and you will need to rub a little well-oiled elbow grease into the muscles of your **Signature Swing** to make it perform smoothly.

The great thing about building something yourself is that you know what's gone into the pie, in the same way as building your own house. You know that you are only using good quality materials; you make sure that the foundations are deep enough to support the building and more besides. As you build your house you check every stage of the process, making sure that you are happy until it is fully built. It might take a little longer to do it this way, this is no short cut, but you can be sure that it will forever stand tall. It may not necessarily tower above the rest but it gives you the great satisfaction of showing the world that you can hold your own.

To be honest nobody else is important here apart from you. If you don't enjoy a little practice and are not really that bothered about improving your golf a lot, then please enjoy your lot. If on the other hand you enjoy a challenge with very realistic goals to keep you on your toes and want to improve then please follow my instructions, we can achieve this together.

Short cuts in life are for the lazy dreamers that may get lucky once, but this never lasts long. If you do it my way, which I know from experience works through filtering out the gold from the garbage with blood, sweat and tears, you will save yourself a lot of precious time and energy, amongst other things. You will no longer have to play catch up like a dog chasing his tail. Why spend your life running around with buckets in a nonsense effort to patch a leaking roof when you can build it properly in the first place?

- Begin practice swinging with your eyes firmly fixed on your target

Signature Golf Swing: Stop fighting with complicated swing mechanics!

- Address your ball dynamically, ready to fire into action with your feet together
- Turn your head only and focus once again on your target
- Turn your head back to your ball and focus on your ball
- Your target is the only thought in your mind's eye

- Let your swing go and react to your target
- Swing back and push the guide ball away or swing over your guide tee without spoiling the party by hitting your single malt

- Maintain your straight left wrist and the extension of your club shaft with your left hand and arm at all times.

Signature Swing: 2nd Gear

- Place your club head into the goalkeeper's hands, he's waiting for it

- Swing down on the line of your guide club slightly to the right of your target, missing your other single malt and unleash your release to fire squarely and smack your target straight between the eyes

Your swing direction is the boss of your swing. Hit the bully straight between the eyes and the bully will never dare raise his ugly head again, if he does, smack him again! When your instincts and feelings have given you the green light you can move up through the gears and introduce your body. Your mastery begins with precision and then (and only then) it's time to unleash your power into your game plan, raging but of course fully under control.

To trust your golf, place it into the hands of a PGA Professional

Eyes wide shut!

Turn the lights off and what are you left with? Feeling and instinct, that's if you don't want to fall flat on your face! To really heighten your senses, promoting even greater awareness of your body movements for exceptional feel and control, leave your eyes wide shut.

It might scare the pants off you at the beginning but with a little trust it's amazing how clever and sophisticated the piece of kit you have lodged between your ears really is. If there's a power cut and the lights go out you have no choice other than to find your way around using your other senses. Again this isn't coming from the mouth of a simpleton like me but from the science boffins with the big foreheads. They have discovered that such exercises are a great way to redirect focus, sharpening your brain's pencil by taking you out of your safety net and making you use your other senses to feel your way around. The results can be extraordinary and after only a few practice sessions your brawn will be in your brains.

Closing your eyes will also prove to you that it's not necessary to have your eyes burning a hole into your ball throughout your swing. If the boss of your swing (1st Gear: Swing Direction) is correct your body will move the way it was made to do so. This is a very effective method of fine tuning and sharpening your instinctive feeling for your **Signature Swing** in relation to your target. The power has gone down, but you need to get to your keys that are sitting on top of your bedside table, what do you naturally do? You picture the layout of your house, work your way to your bedroom and climb over the bed to the keys. What was your main point of focus? Your keys were because without them you wouldn't be able to drive your kids to football practice and you would lose your hero status right there and then.

You may well be thinking, "If my eyes are shut, how am I supposed to react to a target I can't see?" Focus on something now, wherever you are. Close your eyes and visualise the same scene or object that you have just looked at. Your brain has burned an imprint of the information processed by your eyes which you can now see with your mind's eye and your eyes closed. What do most amateur golfers visualise over a ten metre putt? Missing! What should you think about during your journey around the golf course? Your target! Your golf is no longer the same as the average Joe's, my friend.

Now do you see where I am heading with this? This is the secret, this is what all great players either do naturally or work hard at to remove negative thought patterns from their heads, replacing them with positive, more productive stuff. Where is your end goal? Your target! So why would you want to think about anything else? Fill your head with your target so that there is no room for anything else to get in. When you have built your **Signature Swing** and are happily driving in **Top Gear** I will arm you with a Pre-Shot Routine that will pump your body and soul full of positive influences, firing you into your Zone. You will like it; it's a nice quiet place where you are finally and once and for all fully in control.

Your eyes are now wide shut:

- Select your target
- Address your ball dynamically (as detailed during 1st and 2nd Gear)
- Focus on your target
- Focus on the ball
- Close your eyes with only your target in mind
- Let your swing go, react to your target

Close your eyes to sharpen your mind and the secret that great players have known for generations will become crystal clear

To trust your golf, place it into the hands of a PGA Professional

Signature Swing: 3rd Gear

Swing Myth 8: The Tiger effect

Muhammad Ali was the good-looking, smooth-talking Heavy Weight Champion of the World who flew like a butterfly and stung like a bee but his most impressive attribute that made him stand out from the rest was his fancy footwork!

Tiger Woods blasts onto the scene and wins every Major in sight, every part of his swing gets analysed with such intensity that it sends shock waves through the world of golf. Tiger Woods, for those of you that have been living on the moon for a while, is the guy with the red T-shirt and rock solid body that can consistently spin around itself at the speed of light, and that has been doing so since the day he was born. He propelled himself to the top of the game's elite within the blink of an eye, immersed in the secret ingredient every golfer would kill for.

Do you honestly believe that his success has absolutely nothing to do with his phenomenal short game and that it is rather due to the fact that he drives the ball thirty metres longer than the next best guy? The speed of his hip turn has captured the glare of the world's media and has come under the spotlight; his secret has been revealed to every Tom, Dick and Harry. If you believe that if you spin your hips in an attempt to mimic the "Tiger" you will hit the ball further and straighter than ever before then you will be the proud owner of a golf swing that you'll never trust in a month of Sundays.

A typical pupil that wants to generate more power and wants to correct his slice will assure me that the secret to his success lies in the way he moves his hips as he starts his downswing. He will start off with a few practice swings spinning his hips so fast that he almost starts to bore himself into the ground. His main problem, he tells me, is that he has a slice because he has an outside to inside downswing path which is correct and that he is too stiff in his hips.

Downswing incorrectly initiated by the upper body due to swinging the club head to the left of the target, blocking the weight transference and rotation of the body

Signature Golf Swing: Stop fighting with complicated swing mechanics!

At this point I am grinning like a Cheshire Cat! No seriously, his hips are fine; they are a symptom and not a cause of the problem. His swing directional fault is blocking their movement and this will eventually bust his hips open at the same moment as his lower back, as and when his luck decides to run out.

As he gets to the top of his backswing he has two dominant downswing methods. The first, due to his excessive hip turn/spin in the downswing is when his whole body turns with him. This, unbeknown to him, causes his downswing path to come even more from outside to inside, swinging much too far to the left of his target. He now points to his right shoulder and asks me "did you see it?" He believes that his perfectly healthy right shoulder is destroying his downswing. He now has the ability to display a full range of shots from a Slice to a Pull Hook without knowing which one is coming next, or where his ball is heading.

For his next shot he assures me that he will hold his shoulder back somehow and spin his hips even faster which will surely stop his shoulder from coming over the top and resulting in a Slice again. An added bonus he tells me is that his hips will automatically generate more club head speed as he drops his hands down, more on the inside, closer to his body. At some stage he says with a twinkle in his eye and lick of his lips "the driving range will not be long enough for me…"

He then forces his right shoulder back as he starts his downswing, spins his hips, drops the club too far inside and his upper body totally disconnects from his lower, faster-spinning body. He has developed another beautiful range of shots from a Push Slice to a Duck Hook. Guess what? This will cost him a small fortune in ammunition. If he practises long enough his lower back starts to hurt and he wonders why? Be my guest and try to tell him to stop turning his hips this way. Even if you are Tiger this is not the reason Tiger hits the ball so far or why he is the legend that he is, so get over it

Downswing incorrectly initiated by the isolation and increase in speed of the hip rotation, forcing the hands too far inside of plane and disconnecting the co-ordinated movements of the upper and lower body.

Start your downswing with your hips. If you are a seasoned golfer you will have heard these magic words a thousand times. It is crucial to your progress and your natural development that you stop thinking about your hips in your downswing. This is a quick fix that fixes nothing and only adds grey hairs and more problems than a hole in a boat, two wrongs don't make a right. Isolating your hips in your downswing and artificially turning them to mimic the correct movements to improve your downswing is as much use as a car without an engine, you'll be left with an empty shell.

If this is you then please stop believing the rubbish you hear all of the time about fast hips equalling power and accuracy. If your hips are faster than they should be, turning out of sequence with the rest of your body then you will have a totally disconnected and hard to time golf swing. If you are trying to correct your downswing with more hip turn do yourself a favour and stop right now, it doesn't work. You have got a swing path directional problem but it's got nothing to do with your hips. If your shots are starting left of your target take a few steps back, start again and go back to the **Signature Swing** 1st Gear phase to straighten this out until your swing is back on track. Then and only then should you move through the gears. Otherwise let the fight commence until something gets hurt and I don't mean your pride. If you artificially start your downswing with your hips your swing will end up feeling like a jar of onions, in a right pickle.

If you throw a ball with both distance and direction in mind and you miss your target, do you look at your hips or your right shoulder? Take a step back and think about this logically for a moment and relate it to a sport that you have already played, be it football, tennis or whatever. You never think about spinning your hips as you try to hit any ball but in golf, because the ball is not moving, we have chance to analyse the movement to death, pull it to pieces and stick it all back together again.

If your golfing peers promote a faster hip turn please challenge it, they are your hips. Feel free to ask why golf is the only sport you know that as you attack a ball you have to think about how your hips laterally rotate. If you are trying to manipulate the movement of your hips to correct your swing then this is a clear sign and a big flashing red light that something in your swing is not functioning properly, normally indicating a swing directional problem. Forcing your hips to move or rotate in isolation is a waste of your time. Stand up now and throw a ball this way or hit a ball with this in mind. You should simply never even have to give this a second thought, so don't…

You often hear about a boxer having fancy footwork or a tennis or a footballer player for that matter, this is where you should be looking for the secret. Tiger Woods transfers all of his body weight from one side of his body to the other (as do all great powerful golfers) just like a knock-out punch at lightning speed. Tiger Woods has such aggressive hip action as a result of the speed with which he transfers his body weight from one side of his body to the other; it is definitely not down to his hips alone. **Tiger Wood's hips are totally normal like yours and mine and the movement of his hips is part of a chain reaction of natural occurring events that I will prove to you…**

To trust your golf, place it into the hands of a PGA Professional

The Mirror never lies

The truth is; the mirror never lies. That's the reason we all skate past it first thing in a morning without even a peak until we are fully showered, pruned and smelling like a bunch of roses. Or is that just me?

The golf swing is under the continuously watchful eye of the media microscope bounced from one method of madness to the other depending on what and when you read. If you are serious about improving, it starts to play with your head and becomes a challenge in itself, knowing where to look next. The mirror is a good place to start, so if you're a frog lets turn you into a Prince with a swing worthy of a King.

Stand facing the mirror with no ball or club and place your hands together as if you were holding your golf club in your dynamically ready address position. We are now moving away from your 1st and 2nd Gears and up a level to the introduction of your body in the 3rd Gear phase of your **Signature Swing**.

This is really not hip!

- You're standing dynamically ready for action with your feet just inside of shoulder width apart. Your body is now running in one straight line from your feet up to your shoulders.
- Simply swing your hands and arms back and forth mimicking your 1st and 2nd Gear phases of your **Signature Swing** but with no weight transference.

Signature Golf Swing: Stop fighting with complicated swing mechanics!

This is about the time that the untrained eye of the guy wearing those heavily rose-tinted glasses resting on top of his head like a film star figures out that something is not quite as it should be. The running commentary fires into action, "turn your shoulders ninety degrees, turn your hips forty-five degrees, face your back to the target, keep your left arm straight, stick your backside out and for god's sake keep your head down". This guy is trying to teach you an explosive, target orientated sport that thrives on instinct and feeling from a text book. Did you learn how to throw a ball from reading a book, or how to play tennis or ski from a manual?

If you force your body to do something it doesn't want to do it will eventually hate you for it. Complicating a natural movement my friend is the best way to tie yourself up in a knot that will be so difficult to unravel it will blow your head clean off your shoulders.

Do you sit down and analyse your throwing action, take it to bits and put it all back together again? Then do you pick your target thinking about your hips, shoulders, elbow, hand, legs and wrist as you throw your ball? The point that I am trying to make clear here is that most of the things that happen in any movement are part of a chain reaction of naturally occurring events. If the basics are set in place and the movement is started off in the correct way it's like a snowball rolling down a mountain. It starts off small but as it builds momentum gradually develops becoming stronger and faster until it grows into a force of nature to be reckoned with. The day that the snowball falls off the edge of the cliff-face (as happens to all great players from time to time) all that you need to do is to go back to the top of your mountain again, set the basics back in place and watch it build up gradually by itself. Move through the gears and watch the basics roll smoothly into one heck of a force of nature to be reckoned with.

The Man in the mirror: Make a change; it'll feel real good, it'll make a difference!

This is where I get to blow the text book to shreds and show you how your body naturally turns, moves and hinges, the way it was made to do.

- You're standing dynamically ready for action with your feet just inside of shoulder width apart. Your body is now running in one straight line from your feet up to your shoulders
- Swing your arms away as you would in your backswing and at the same time smoothly shift the majority of your body weight onto your right foot
- Swing your hands and arms back down as you would in your downswing and at the same time smoothly shift the majority of your body weight onto your left foot
- Allow your body to naturally turn, as in your follow through over your left foot, balanced and supported by the toes of your right foot

Signature Swing: 3rd Gear

This is how your golf swing works and fits naturally with the way you were made to move. This is how your body generates power from your body mass when you throw a ball, kick a ball or play tennis. You have been doing it this way all of your life, so why stop now? If you move too far across to your right side in your backswing, guess what? You'll lose your balance, so don't. Try to maintain a well-balanced and nicely centred body throughout your swing, with your head sitting proudly on your shoulders as was intended.

If you throw a ball, as you draw the ball back you load the majority of your body weight onto your right foot. As you head back to the target with your ball hand your body weight transfers over to your left side smoothly, moving across as you release your ball, eventually finishing fully loaded onto your left side.

You are throwing the ball with your full body mass behind it, in doing so you are making the most of the biggest weapon in your artillery, you of course. This is no different to a golf swing so put the text book down, tell the running commentary to put a sock in it and find the nearest mirror. Please put my theory to the test and see with your own two eyes how the weight transference rotates your body with ease, without pain and without thinking of one hundred swing thoughts.

Get hold of a golf club, don't worry the chandelier is not in danger because in 3rd Gear you are only aiming for a half swing at approximately waist height. You can tell your wife/husband (or mum/dad) that everything is under control. Your 1st and 2nd Gears will guide your body into position as you gently introduce your weight transference into the equation.

Do this with lightning speed with highly honed co-ordination and I can assure you that your hips will look like Tigers. The only thing that is missing is the bit in the middle; the millions of hours of practice, so don't start beating yourself up just yet.

To trust your golf, place it into the hands of a PGA Professional

Signature Swng: 3rd Gear half swing; Body

Muhammad Ali was right on all accounts in the sporting arena. This is why he was the best of the best, The Champion of the World. He knew that to be powerful and unbeatable he had to fly around the ring like a butterfly to sting like a bee. He knew better than to throw himself head first into the fight, this is too dangerous for any man. He knew he had to move smoothly and be light on his feet to deliver the killer blow. The man was a genius...

What can you learn from the legend Muhammad Ali? A lot!! This is the best way to build your golf swing or to play any sport for that matter. To generate power you have to be light on your feet. Your movements have to be smoothly co-ordinated in order for you to sting like a bee. If you force a shot by hitting too hard in tennis what happens? What about in football? If you kick a ball at full force the ball finishes in the stands and puts you flat on your back, the same can be said for golf, it is no different.

You are now ready to move up to 3rd Gear to further build up your **Signature Swing**. By now you fully understand that power comes from a smooth, well-performed technique, so please don't throw yourself head first into the fight. Slowly build your Signature Swing. Feel your body weight transfer smoothly within the natural rotation, firmly planted and well balanced onto your right foot in your backswing then across onto your left foot in your forward swing. If you lose your balance it is a clear indication that you are swaying from side to side too much, maintain your body's natural centre of gravity without moving/swinging like a wooden man.

In **Posture: Alive and kicking** and **1st Gear: Backswing** achieving a dynamic and well balanced body in your golf swing is highly dependent upon the relationship between the centre of gravity of your body (the base of your spine) and the centre of gravity of your swing (the base of your neck). Throughout your **Signature Swing** it is essential that these two points of centre of gravity that were automatically set at address by the *drop* remain in harmonic balance. If at any given point during your swing their relationship changes then it will directly affect the positioning of your spine angle either lifting your upper body back and up out of the shot or forcing you to arch your back, both scenarios resulting in a blocked body rotation. The full significance of the important role that this plays in the effectiveness of your **Signature Swing** will be fully explained soon on your way up to **Top Gear** in **Core Rotation**

A word of warning, don't be rocking and rolling all over the place. You need fancy footwork to fly like a butterfly and sting like a bee so stop walking the plank like a drunken sailor. Let your weight transference flow from one foot to the other, your body will react accordingly, freely rotating and being guided by your hands and arms swinging back and forth on the correct swing path in relation to your target.

The 3rd Gear build up phase of your **Signature Swing** is a half swing at approximately waist height. Please don't hop, skip and jump before you can walk, you will lose so much ground if you do. Have a target for every shot that you play, if you don't you will have nothing to learn.

Please use all of your guides; they are in place for a reason. Don't let yourself down by being complacent, you will pay the price for slipping into bad habits forcing your swing into your **Golf Swing Danger Zone**, it's not worth it. It's about time you took control and placed your finger well and truly on the pulse of your game.

- Begin practise swinging with your eyes fixed firmly on your target (target view)

Signature Swing: 3rd Gear

- Begin practise swinging with your eyes fixed firmly on your target (side view)

- Address your ball dynamically, ready to fire into action with your feet just under shoulder width apart
- Turn your head only and focus once again on your target

- Turn your head back to your ball and focus on your ball
- Your target is the only thought in your mind's eye

Signature Golf Swing: Stop fighting with complicated swing mechanics!

- Let your swing go and react to your target
- Swing back and push the guide ball away or swing over your guide tee without spoiling the party by hitting your single malt. As you do, transfer your body weight smoothly onto your right foot

- Maintain your straight left wrist and the extension of your club shaft with your left hand and arm at all times. Place your club head into the goalkeeper's hands, he's waiting for it. Feel your body weight loaded but light on your right foot, ready to smoothly move in the opposite direction in your downswing

- Swing down on the line of your guide club, slightly to the right of your target, incorporating your release and smoothly transfer your body weight across onto your left foot.
- As you continue down through the impact area and into your follow through your weight transference has shifted further onto your left foot. Your release is working as one with your swing direction, presenting a square clubface in relation to your target at impact and shortly thereafter

www.golfswingzone.com

Signature Swing: 3rd Gear

- Allow your head to turn with your body into your follow through just after your impact position to finish looking in the direction of your target.
- Into your follow through and beyond make sure that your follow through single malt is still standing tall. The momentum and direction of your swing will guide the natural rotation of your body, finishing with the majority of your body weight firmly planted on your left foot. Allow your right foot to naturally turn to support your rotation and weight shift by finishing balanced up onto your toes

You have added a new dimension to your **Signature Swing**. You have started to pile on the muscle, beefing up your main swing foundation as the boss of your swing (swing direction) carries more clout. Your ball will start to naturally fly further but this is not your goal here. Precision and control come before anything so leave the hero at home for a while and gradually build on your technique, instinctively firing at your target.

I appreciate that it is difficult in the early stages to be instinctive and to react whilst you are learning the new physical movements of your **Signature Swing**. Your target is your guiding light. As you gradually grow in confidence and your muscles adjust, co-ordinating the new swing movements, you can move closer eventually playing exclusively in your target orientated mind-set. As it all comes together the secrets the golfing greats have known for generations (reacting with only your target in mind) will give you the green light, ready to move up to another gear.

Be patient and invest time to allow yourself to develop your instinct and feeling for the co-ordination in the early stages of your swing. I can guarantee that you will reap the long-term benefits, paying dividends in your golfing future. Please do not move up a gear until you have mastered this stage of your **Signature Swing**.

To trust your golf, place it into the hands of a PGA Professional

Signature Swing: 4th Gear

Swing Myth 9: Perfectly still and 90

This is something that is promoted and taught on a regular basis on fairways and driving ranges all over the world. If you know anyone who can keep their head perfectly still and can turn their shoulders ninety degrees then you are either looking at a very flexible person or possibly an owl.

Throughout the development of any physical movement that is part of a sport there are three rules of thumb that I am convinced about. The first is never fight with Mother Nature, you will never win. You are who you are, you can improve on it but hanging from a tree all night long won't make your arms significantly longer. The second is don't force your body to do something when it's screaming out at you that it doesn't like it, it will only end in tears. The third is if someone recommends that you should move your body in such a way as to benefit the sport you are playing but you don't understand the reason why then question it. If there is no reasonably viable answer apart from, "that's just the way it is" then the person you are talking to is shuffling around in his shoes now feeling a little out of his depth. To take it one step further if you feel the advice that you are being given is particularly poor and unhelpful ask that the same person to do it first. If he can't turn his shoulders ninety degrees and keep his head perfectly still then how can he expect you to improve being taught this way?

If you have a mirror at hand, face it and keep your head perfectly still whilst rotating your shoulders however you like as long as you reach a ninety degree angle of turn.

Now give it a go and make an extra special effort to keep your lower body quiet and your hips still. To give it an extra boost, try to turn your left shoulder over your right foot

A perfectly still head blocking weight transference and body rotation

In turning your left shoulder over your right foot your head is forced to move too far across to the right, with your upper body

This is the rose-tinted glasses guy again firing his useless text book running commentary over your shoulder. If you don't give him his marching orders he may be the only form of transport you have to get you to Accident and Emergency to pop your disc back in. This is serious stuff and not for the faint hearted, it's your life!

As far as I know all of this coiling your upper body against your lower body originates way back to the golfing legend Ben Hogan. He wrote a book that is still referred to, to this day, by experts in the golfing world. Mr Hogan was renowned as a perfectionist who was never happy with his swing so he took it to bits and put it all back together again, as did the great Nick Faldo who displayed similar traits. It is not easy to suck all of the life, feeling and instincts out of your swing, rebuild it with foreign parts and inject instinct and feeling, breathing life back into it successfully. I personally have wasted many an hour taking ten steps backwards and five to the side into a ditch in the middle of nowhere. Mr Hogan and Mr Faldo were very gifted, determined and actually unstoppable. Mr Faldo won the British Open and sang, "I did it my way", but to be honest I think he would have done it anyway.

To get back to the point, all of this coiling and winding up of your upper body against your lower body in an attempt to create tension that when fully loaded will fire you out at tremendous speed like a catapult is very misleading. For a start what feels hot to one man can feel lukewarm to another. A limited amount of tension is often necessary but to build up to bursting point as is often portrayed to the guy on the street is useless. Being tense or allowing a build-up of tension in the body during any physical task is often rightly described as being a disadvantage. Your body, when it is tense, has either been pushed too far or the occasion is hindering your performance. If you don't believe me, screw a piece of paper up and throw it at an easy target. Rockefeller comes along and offers you a cool million if you can do the same again. I didn't see you sweating first time. That's tension messing with you. Your body does not have the same capacity as an elastic band, it will snap, especially if you push it too far with Perfectly Still and 90.

Perhaps there was an underlying reason for Mr Hogan to re-build his swing this way, to fit his own body and the way it performed best, did anyone ask him? It worked for him as history speaks for him and his technique loud and clear, the man was one of the greatest. It would be interesting to have known if he felt that his swing was too loose, with his hands and arms disconnecting, straying away from his body. Maybe his body often felt unstable during his swing, especially under pressure, so the answer for him was to tighten the screw, coil and feel the tension. This is just an idea, but I guess we'll never really know.

I am totally convinced that a powerful golf swing is not tense but that it rather consists of a rotation around a well centred core. Body mass transfers from one side to the other, guided by the direction of the target and the force created in the transition from backswing to forward swing is fully utilised. The natural force created in the transition phase maximises the dynamics of your **Signature Swing**, I will get to this shortly. A big hitter in the ring throws his weight around, but if he throws his arms too far away from his body's centre of gravity he'll lose balance and leave himself wide open to all kinds of punishment. A powerfully pure golf swing or any explosive, target orientated sport correctly executed will vouch for me on this one, it's no different. Are you tense when you throw a ball to a distant target?

For you to naturally rotate around your core and to ensure that you are working within the limits of your centre of gravity during your golf swing, your head will move slightly from side to side as it does when you play tennis, throw a ball or play any sport for that matter. The problem only occurs when your head moves out of your centre of gravity. If you play a tennis shot and your head is behind your body, this forces your body weight back onto your heels, resulting in a high right shot landing in the next court. Golf is no exception. As with most sports your head is naturally positioned on top of your body, over your body for a reason. If you stand up and lean forward the weight of your head takes your body with it, this is the reason you should always work within your body's natural centre of gravity. Your head should not be still or wooden nor too far down or up, simply naturally in place as intended over your body.

If the guy with the rose-tinted glasses highly recommends that you turn your back to the target and keep your head still, then go for an early shower. If anyone places a club shaft to your chest in an attempt to explain to you how your upper body rotates, don't come out of the shower until he's gone. If you were taught to play tennis or football and someone held a stick to your chest in a vain attempt to tell you how your body should rotate would you take him seriously? These are gimmicks that look and sound great but only to the untrained eye of the poor guy at the sharp end of the stick, which is no longer you my friend...

To trust your golf, place it into the hands of a PGA Professional

Signature Swing: Core rotation

A powerful and controlled golf swing is a golf swing that is rotated, well centred within its weight lines, naturally around its core. If you imagine a hammer thrower, a baseball player, a tennis player or any sport that has something thrown or hit from a standing position, the rotation and build-up of power within the rotation is the secret.

Many golfers are totally obsessed and brainwashed into believing that a golf swing is not a golf swing unless you are constantly battling with your hip or shoulder turn. Golf is no different to any other explosive, target orientated sport as far is the production of controlled power is concerned. I have said time and again that your body rotates and moves as part of a chain reaction of events guided by the direction of your swing as you transfer your body weight. If your swing is poorly directed then your body and natural rotation will be blocked. That is a cold, hard fact whether you like it or not. If you are sucked in (as many are), you may try in vain to isolate a body part, such as your shoulders, turning them in front of a mirror until the cows eventually come home...correcting nothing and over stretching something at best.

In **Posture: Alive and Kicking** and **1ˢᵗ Gear: Backswing** achieving a dynamic and well balanced body in your golf swing is highly dependent on the relationship between the centre of gravity of your body (the base of your spine) and the centre of gravity of your swing (the base of your neck). Throughout your **Signature Swing** it is essential that these

www.golfswingzone.com

Signature Swing: 4th Gear

two points of centre of gravity that were automatically set at address by the *drop* remain in harmonic balance. If at any given point during your swing their relationship changes then it will directly affect the positioning of your spine angle either lifting your upper body back and up, out of the shot or forcing you to arch your back, both scenarios resulting in a blocked body rotation.

This is often a topic of confusion as many are misinformed or have never really bothered to study it in any great depth. The "stiff, straight spine angle" is over preached, a total misinterpretation of a natural position which you automatically achieve as you flick your switch into sports mode and *drop* into position. If you try to force a body part to remain stiff you are blocking it and therefore any natural movement that it is no longer free to make. This runs through your body like an express train eventually blocking everything you have!

As you build your **Signature Swing** you begin the process with your feet together to simplify the movement until you have learned to master the *boss* (swing direction) of your *half* swing. Once the *boss* has taken charge and is in total control of your swing it is then that it is mature enough to take the strain of your whole body. The *boss* of your swing, with the help of the correct use of weight transference, guides the natural rotation of your body resulting in a consistent and well co-ordinated *half* swing. Your club head, as you complete your backswing, sits slap bang in the middle of the goal keeper's hands which are positioned in the centre of gravity for your swing, in line with the base of your neck. You will be safe in the knowledge that your follow through is well directed at your target because your best teacher, the *ball*, has told you so.

The lollipop lady has watched you like a hawk as you safely crossed the road with your own two feet, one step at a time, as I promised you that you would all along. "Cometh the moment, cometh the man", it is time for you to take your **Signature Swing** all the way to **Top Gear** This is where many a man has fallen flat on his face in a pile of mess and confusion in a vain effort to try to stick his golf swing and all of its over promoted complex components together whilst ignoring the simple things in life.

The shoes that you stand in today were made to fit you perfectly, so to stand in someone else's shoes doesn't add up. There are some simple laws of physics that cannot be ignored whatever your make or model! The swift changing of gears on the way up to **Top Gear,** as you lengthen your **Signature Swing** from half swing to full, may well be brimming with unpleasant surprises and full of disappointment if you fight with your biomechanics and the way that you were skilfully crafted.

The *core* is the middle of your body, your heart and soul and where your natural balancing mechanisms function at their best. If your movement or a body part strays too far away from its core, your body will have to adjust and compensate to support it, spending valuable energy in the process. Your body is most receptive to and performs most physical tasks best within its core and centre of gravity. You are well armed to create the energy and power from within your rotating core by using the natural radius and arc of your arms during your swing. These are your natural tools.

Imagine a discus thrower spinning himself around, generating power from within his core rotation. The natural forces that he creates from this rotation run up his arm, shooting directly to the furthest point from his core, his hand. When the power is at its strongest and he can no longer hold back he releases the discus, propelling it into the distance. The discus thrower uses the spinning motion to create his power. **In golf, tennis, baseball or just when throwing a ball, it is the combination of weight transference and arm swing direction in relation to your target that produces the natural rotation around your body's core. This is where the power is generated.**

The moment that the centre of gravity of your body (the base of your spine) and the centre of gravity of your swing (the base your neck) are removed from their harmonic balanced state much of the power and control that your body creates will vanish into thin air, so be warned! As you lengthen your **Signature Swing** from half to full swing, however long or short your arms or legs are or however big your head is for that matter it is essential that the positioning of these two points remains the same throughout.

The *drop* as in **Posture: Alive and Kicking** automatically flicked your switch into sport mode. The bending/flexing of your knees at the same time as you leaned forward with your shoulders naturally squeezed your hips out pushing your backside out with them. Your back and therefore your spine angle was set in its optimum position ready to take the strain of whatever you were about to throw at it. The moment the relationship between the base of your spine and the base of your neck changes so does your spine angle leaving your discs wide open for a good hiding! Ignoring the simple laws of physics not only comes with a health warning but with a golf warning loaded with weak and inconsistent shots. A change in your spine angle at any stage in your golf swing is a one way ticket to fairways from hell and to miserable, weak and painful golf!

Firstly I want to stress that the rotation is heavily dependent on your physical capabilities. This is not necessarily age, as I have learnt from experience... Some seventy year old players can turn around themselves like a spinning top. You will only be able to turn or rotate as far as your body dictates. Forcing your body into positions that it doesn't want to be in will cause injury and will negatively affect your golf. You have to work with what you have. If you're not happy with your lot then you have to work on what you've got. I will show you how to improve your range of motion and how to prepare to perform at your best shortly.

The natural weight lines in your Signature Swing

To complement your **Core Rotation** there are two vital weight lines that many of explosive, target orientated sports naturally use to maximise the true dynamics of the movements involved. The weight lines run from the inside of your right heel up through your right shoulder and vice versa from the inside of your left heel up through your left shoulder.

- As you reach the end of your backswing your left shoulder meets the weight line that runs from inside of your right heel up through your right shoulder
- As you finish your forward swing your right shoulder meets the weight line that runs from inside of your left heel up through your left shoulder

If your golf swing is working outside of your weight lines it doesn't matter how great the other aspects of your swing are, you are trapped in a fight for composure to regain balance every time that you play. You are losing more distance than you can dream to imagine and your consistency is being shot to pieces. You are fighting with Mother Nature and you are losing big time.

If you have ever tried to isolate your rotation in an attempt to improve it you have been wasting your time, blindly lead by the blind. Crossing your hands over your chest or placing a club shaft parallel to your shoulders to imitate the rotating process is probably, at best, stretching something. These exercises are totally useless because a rotation in your golf swing is part of a natural chain reaction of events guided into position by the boss of your swing, the direction your hands and arms are swinging in, in relation to your target.

If you were waiting for your tennis partner to get changed you wouldn't stand in the locker room with your arms crossed over your chest, turning your upper body to see if it's rotating as it should. If you were to do anything you would mimic the shot in your mind's eye at an imaginary target using the combination of your tennis stroke direction and the transference of your body weight. Hey presto, your body naturally rotates within your centre of gravity.

This is not a newly found secret system I'm exposing here, this is the way our bodies have moved and reacted since the day cavemen realised that if they were not a crack shot they would go hungry. If your hands and arms are swinging in the wrong direction your natural rotation and weight transference will be blocked. That means that isolating your rotation in an attempt to perfect it has no bearing on your golf swing. As you are now fully aware from the 1st Gear phase of your **Signature Swing**, your swing direction is the boss of your swing, guiding its natural rotation in relation to the direction of your target. You have the most advanced computer at your fingertips. If you use it and program it to do the things that it is good at, it will do the job for you.

We are all (thankfully) built individually and nobody's perfect with various strengths and weaknesses that come with the year and make of the model. There is no production line turning out perfect golf swings either and a one size fits all

Signature Swing: 4th Gear

usually involves an elastic waist band that only looks good on a pregnant lady, at most. A golf swing on the other hand is an athletic, explosive, rhythmic movement that flows gracefully when fuelled with instinct and feeling. You are at the crucial stages on your way up to your **Top Gear** so it's about time that you forgot the brainwashing, dangerous, time wasting stuff and concentrated on building your own **Signature Swing** the way it should be built. By this I mean from the ground up on a solid foundation, by the most important golfer in your world, with the exclusive use of your own two hands.

Your **Signature Swing** building process is gradually increasing in response to your own feeling and progression as you move up through the gears from your half swing to full. A gradual building process will arm you with a greater awareness of your body parts in relation to your target, co-ordinating your own individual swing. This has many advantages, the main one being that you are building your own swing from the ground up. You know what goes into the pie so you can make it again. If the green light glows then don't hesitate, go on. If it's on amber, be patient a little longer and with more practice great things will happen.

A sequence of naturally occurring events turns your body automatically around your core, in relation to your target.

To trust your golf, place it into the hands of a PGA Professional

Swing Myth 10: The Biggest cock-up

If you think that you have already wasted too much time and energy searching for the secret or the magic move that will rock your golfing world, I'm sure I could give you a run for your money, actually any day of the week. The last swing myth I'm going to demolish is something that I spent a lot of time practising, drilling into my bones with bucket after bucket of balls. It was only later as my career took a new direction into the coaching arena that I discovered the reason that my golf swing was at times difficult to control, and this would come totally out of the blue. It became a personal quest to discover where it all went wrong and how I could prevent the same thing happening to another strong ambition with bright eyes and a firm hold on a distant dream.

It may shock you to learn this is something that is taught and that comes highly recommended by many top flight coaches, however I believe that it is the biggest downward spiral that any golfer of any standard can fall into. This swing myth has credentials that come with a gold stamp and is thought key and fundamental to the building process of a golf swing. It's actually regarded as one of the main swing elements that supposedly generates power and precision. I can say with a lump in my throat that this is the biggest, over-rated cock-up of all time and that it will destroy a golf swing in a matter of minutes.

Setting your hands at the top of your backswing with hinging, cocking or breaking of your wrists will leave you permanently fighting with a golf swing that you wouldn't trust in a month of Sundays. Without trust what are you left with? I trained my wrist hinge in my backswing for years, in the belief that it would improve my golf, but the more that I practised the more of an issue that the clubface alignment at the top of my backswing became.

Early hinge, mid hinge and late hinge were all things that my swing became familiar with, unbeknown to me this was the main reason that my golf swing would work fantastically one day and spray all over the park the next.

Swing sequence showing early wrist hinge in the backswing

Signature Golf Swing: Stop fighting with complicated swing mechanics!

Swing sequence showing mid wrist hinge in the backswing

Swing sequence showing late wrist hinge in the backswing

If you hinge, break or cock your wrists at any stage in your backswing your straight left wrist angle will be broken. It is essential that a straight left wrist is in place at the top of your backswing for your clubface to be square and parallel to your left forearm. As in my case, which is the most common result of a wrist hinge in a backswing, your left wrist will naturally cup and your clubface will be wide open. If you are not aware of the underlying root cause of the problem, which is the hinge itself, you will do as I did and slap a plaster on to try to square your clubface angle by using the opposite wrist movement and arch your left wrist at a later stage in your backswing. These two wrongs will beat your feelings and instincts to a pulp.

This leaves you in a very vulnerable position especially when the heat is turned up a notch and those nerve endings start to jingle. Hinging your wrists opens your clubface, cupping your left wrist. Arching your left wrist towards the top of your backswing closes your clubface in the hope that your clubface will be square when it gets there. Yes I said in hope, every dog has his day but not every day and not every shot. If you were to put me on the spot and make me name the most important fundamental that must be in place for a golf swing to be consistent and powerful I wouldn't hesitate for a second. The clubface must be squarely aligned throughout a golf swing in relation to the ball and the target. The number one key element that the majority of great golf swings have in common is a square clubface. If this breaks down then so do all of the other key angles and rotations, one by one, until you are left looking through your fingers in despair. Without a square clubface a golf swing will have to dance around to find the best artificial compensation it can, forcing you closer to your **Golf Swing Danger Zone** and costing you many a wasted hour of precious time and energy.

A good golf swing is not lucky, after all you can only be lucky for so long. A good golf swing has a well-proportioned solid base to work up from and a few key elements that are required to create power, consistency and control. The key elements are: *a dynamic foundation* on which to build, a correct *swing direction* in relation to your target and *clubface alignment* that is true to your swing direction and square in relation to your ball and target. The beef is added at the end with a naturally rotated *body* around its *core*. This is the reason your swing direction and clubface alignment have to be nicely gelled together before you introduce your body. If your swing direction or clubface alignment is wrong then it's down to your body to try to repair the damage which believe me, doesn't work for long, if at all.

Signature Swing: 4th Gear

Every element that goes into a golf swing can be clearly explained, there is an answer to every question, if not then you're firing your question in the wrong direction. How can I prove to you that your wrist hinge in your backswing is affecting the angle of your left wrist causing it to break, opening or closing your clubface?

- Grip your golf club in the centre of your body, then hold your hands out in front of your body
- With still arms move your club shaft vertically up and down, then stop

- With still arms move your club shaft laterally side to side

From this simple exercise you can clearly see that your wrists have little flexibility to move vertically up and down but can move freely laterally from side to side. When related to your backswing this clearly shows that your wrists don't have much room to hinge or cock, although there is a high risk that your wrists will move from side to side, cupping or arching.

A square clubface with a straight flat left wrist | An open clubface with a cupped left wrist | A closed clubface with an arched left wrist

www.golfswingzone.com

Signature Golf Swing: Stop fighting with complicated swing mechanics!

As I have explained, the golf swing that you are trying to build is a natural rotation around its core using the forces naturally generated by your body weight. Your body naturally rotates as you transfer your body weight so the last thing you would want to do is break at the wrists and break the motion. This is an artificial, over-taught, meaningless often painful movement. Anything that is hinged is hinged away from its main body weakening it, so this also makes it more vulnerable and more susceptible to damage.

It's a fact. If you hinge, break or cock your wrists in your backswing then one of the key elements in your backswing breaks down; that is a straight, flat left wrist at the top of your backswing. This mainly results in a cupped left wrist with an open clubface or very possibly an arched left wrist with a closed clubface; neither is more favourable. The breakdown of the left wrist angle during your backswing will also pull your hand and arm out of its natural alignment which is dangerous under the force of your backswing. This will result in stretching of muscles and tendons which ultimately will be felt by you somewhere down the long and winding road.

As you have already discovered from the exercise above, your left wrist will flex slightly although this should never be a conscious effort on your part. If you try to block your wrists or any body part for that matter your golf swing will become stiff, wooden and all of the life blood, *instinct* and *feeling* will be swiftly removed. The weight of the club head on the outside of your swing arc in your backswing will naturally place forces onto your wrists which will make them flex which is fine. The flexing of your wrists should be kept to a minimum so as not to disrupt the alignment of your flat, straight left wrist but you can't put a number on this as what's not enough for one man is plenty for the next. Without doubt the principle of maintaining a *flat, straight wrist* at the top of your backswing is vital to the success of your **Signature Swing**. If there is one element that can make or break you then this is certainly it!

Your wrists do hinge, the guy with the rose-tinted glasses has a point, but he doesn't know where to point to, that's the problem. They hinge as a result of the natural forces placed on them during your swing, in the transition from your backswing into your downswing. The underlying natural force, when fully understood, adds a completely new set of dynamics to your **Signature Swing** as you reach your **Top Gear**.

The only way to be sure that you have a square clubface throughout your backswing is to firstly make sure that you grip your golf club from the one o'clock position, which sets your left wrist and arm as an extension of your club shaft

If you grip the club from the centre of your body your straight left wrist is broken there and then, so don't do it!

Once your grip, wrist and golf club shaft are in line take it all the way up to the top this way. This means that you start with a straight left wrist and square clubface. Take it to the top, maintaining its position and finish with a straight left wrist with a square clubface parallel to your left forearm at the top

It's a guarantee, not a lottery!

To trust your golf, place it into the hands of a PGA Professional

Signature Swing: The Power in transition

To truly maximise the dynamics of your golf swing it is essential that you understand the power of transition. The key to power and exceptional ball striking lies in the transition from backswing to forward swing.

Signature Swing: 4th Gear

The transition phase in a golf swing is often misunderstood, complicated and broken down with individual body parts taking the lead, moving in isolation. The guy with the rose-tinted glasses promotes that you initiate your downswing with your hips and/or left hand which in my mind is totally artificial because it breaks the free flowing movement that produces the natural forces in the first place.

As you are now fully aware the core rotation and weight transference of a great swing (your **Signature Swing** included) is guided by your swing direction in relation to your target. There is a combination of events that manoeuvres your body; it's certainly not a single body part in isolation. Anything isolated is weak because it's working independently and not as a part of the whole package, which together packs a bigger punch.

When you throw a ball you never isolate your hips to start the forward motion. They appear to begin the motion as they do in a golf swing but if this is done in isolation, without the other combined elements, the movement is useless. If you are trying to perfect your throwing action by isolating your hip rotation, you are wasting your time because the natural weight transference does this for you. I will never understand teaching methods that mimic physical movements inherited by the sport in question when they occur as part of the natural motion involved in the movement. I have seen many a golfer standing on the driving range messing around with his hips or pulling down with his left hand in isolation, wasting yet another precious hour of his free time.

Throwing a ball; correct automatic transfer of body weight begins with the lower body

Something which really helped me to understand how the power can be maximised during the transition phase in a golf swing is the action of flicking a towel. You hold the towel by one of the corners. You then pull the towel back, moving it in a direction away from the target. To maximise the power of transition you smoothly but sharply change direction back towards the target. There is a delay as the built up energy during the transition from backward to forward motion travels down the full length of the towel until it reaches the opposite end. It is now that the forces are released as a whipping snap at the point of impact.

The creation of a whipping motion with the flick of a towel (side view)

Signature Golf Swing: Stop fighting with complicated swing mechanics!

The creation of a whipping motion with the flick of a towel (front view)

If you are a tennis player this is no different to a well performed serve. This is how the big servers generate so much power and ball flight speed by utilising the transition from backward to forward motion. This can be best described as a whipping or flicking motion, directly at the point of impact. If you are a fisherman and you pull your rod backwards and then forwards to propel your hook far out into the water to catch the bigger fish, you will firstly feel a delay until the natural force travels the full length of your rod, releasing the forces at the tip of the rod, giving you the same whipping sensation that generates the power.

This force, when maximised and used in your correctly built **Signature Swing**, will change the way you play golf forever. This is the reason good players hit the ball further with a more penetrating ball flight that cuts through the wind like a hot knife through butter.

Most amateur golfers do not use this energy, in fact in most cases it is quite the opposite. There is an obvious giveaway that sticks out like a sore thumb when a golfer doesn't know how to optimise the dynamics of their golf swing. As they start their downswing the arc that is created is long as their wrists open out, hinging away from their body, finishing with a short follow through as they pull their hands and arms into their body. This is either caused by a swing plane problem or simply a lack of knowledge. If you were to look at this swing from the side, facing the front of their body you would clearly see the long downswing arc and short follow-through arc.

The long to short downswing arc created by the opening of the wrists from the top of the backswing and throughout the downswing

Subsequently the long to short swing arc produces less club head speed, less power and problems with the impact position. The opening of the wrist hinge causes problems at impact such as topping the ball or hitting the ground before impact. The most powerful point in the downswing is well before the club head gets down to hit the ball.

Signature Swing: 4th Gear

A word of warning

If your address position is not dynamic and/or your swing direction and clubface are not well aligned in relation to your target you cannot start to pack on the muscle with your body. Your 1st and 2nd Gear phases of your **Signature Swing** will signal you the green light to introduce your 3rd Gear Body phase. If it's not working as it should, putting your foot down on the gas by introducing the power and natural force of the transition phase too soon will lead to your whole swing falling apart piece by piece. This will be clearly seen on the face of your best teacher, your ball of course.

It is no different to improving any explosive, target orientated sport. You learn the basics and build up through the basics until they become your own. At that moment you can release the natural forces that are produced, powerfully and well aligned. If you have a weak link in your **Signature Swing** then it will show its face if you introduce the force of transition too soon, with poorly struck erratic golf shots. Your **Signature Swing** is a gradual building process and cannot just be thrown together in one shot. Feeling and instincts grow, they can't be bought or borrowed.

Feel the power of transition

A simple way to feel how the wrist hinge works in the transition phase is as follows:

- Grip your golf club correctly from the one o'clock position
- Hold your hands out in front of your body

- Swing your golf club at just above waist height around your body as you would with a baseball swing
- With firm, tension free wrists gradually increase the speed of the swing
- As you begin the forward swing you will feel your wrists give, due to the change in direction

This is the wrist hinge, break or cock that is often misunderstood and complicated on countless driving ranges throughout the world. **As you change direction from backswing to forward swing the natural forces, which are strongest at the end of the arc, place pressure on your wrists. They then have no choice but to give**

Signature Golf Swing: Stop fighting with complicated swing mechanics!

way. The power is naturally forced onto the furthest point from your centre of gravity (core). If the motion is broken or paused the natural forces that are generated from within the transition from backswing to forward swing are lost. To maximise the dynamics of your **Signature Swing** your aim is to have your backswing and forward swing become one, in a smooth, flowing movement.

In the transition your wrists give and the club head lags behind your forward swing, actually moving in the opposite direction for a split second. This is often referred to as the Late Hit. Eventually your club head will have to be redirected, following your hands and arms until the stored energy can no longer be contained within your downswing. This energy then shoots to the furthest point away from your core, your hands. The energy created forces your wrists to act within a powerful whipping motion, propelling your club head towards your ball with great power, weight and speed. This is the reason a slightly built golfer can still hit the ball a great distance by utilising the full dynamics of his swing to the max.

The optimal use of swing dynamics in a downswing created naturally by the change in direction from backswing to forward swing

A great way to enhance the feeling of lag is to place more weight at your club head end; there are many readily available devices that fit onto your club head to add weight. The added weight will place even more force onto your wrists in the transition from backswing to forward swing, exaggerating the feeling that you are striving for.

It is possible to manufacture this movement with only the use of your hands and arms as is often attempted and explained by the guy with the rose-tinted glasses sitting on the end of his nose, with no success. This just doesn't work. It's like strawberries without the cream or like listening to your dear Uncle Billy doing his Frank Sinatra; it just doesn't have the same kick. Artificially manufacturing the transition will leave your golf swing limp and useless with your hands and arms flapping around all over the show, opening and closing your clubface.

With practice you will develop a feeling for the transition of your body weight from backswing to forward swing and for the wrist hinge as they naturally give. At first it is a strange kind of delayed sensation until your wrists can no longer contain the angle created by the natural break or hinge. It is then that your club head is propelled powerfully in the direction of your ball. This naturally creates a steeper, sharper descent in your downswing, producing a crisper and cleaner ball strike. This is often the reason that **Swing Myth 3: Hitting down on the ball** is so often misunderstood. You cannot manufacture a natural occurrence successfully and it certainly cannot be taught artificially.

Your wrists cock, hinge or break naturally as a result of the momentum of the change in direction (transition) from backswing to forward swing. This creates a whipping sensation, optimizing the true dynamics of your golf swing.

To trust your golf, place it into the hands of a PGA Professional

Drive to top gear

To drive all the way up to your **Top Gear** the green light must be shining brightly as your instincts in your first three gears are all revved up. The three pearls of wisdom below will have guided you exclusively over to your target orientated zone, pushing your instincts and feelings to their limit until you fully own your first three gears. If you've not quite made the cross-over and you still feel as though you're walking on egg shells be patient, stay focused and allow your guides and target to hold your hand until great things start to happen. You are the man with his finger on the pulse and it's ultimately your decision that counts. **One word of warning;** the only person you are going to cheat out of a successful **Signature Swing** is yourself my friend, so don't!

- Focus on your target
- Focus on your ball
- React to your target (hit the ball)

I have known many a **Signature Swing** to get this far and then fail, not because the techniques don't work but because the owner starts to get sloppy and careless. You have built the main foundation and body of your **Signature Swing**, but this is by no means time to get complacent. You have gained full control over the boss of your swing your swing direction, marrying it together with your club head and you have started the beefing up process by introducing your body. The last thing you want to start doing is unpicking all of the hard work that has got you here.

You have no excuses; you have your guides and controls to keep you on the straight and narrow and to get the job done with intent and conviction, you deserve it. If you are not spending your practice time fully in a controlled environment then you are about to be slapped with a big eye opener. This is where the downward spiral of chasing your tail every time you play starts to kick off the battle between you and your clubface. If you are not being controlled you will need someone with you who you can trust to teach you how to improve. If you want to do it off your own back then you need to be guided. If you are fed up with the control freaks placed on the ground for every practice session then the time has come for us to part company. To be honest without the use of a controlled strategy any success that you achieve if any at all will be very limited and short lived.

Do you think the best players in the world head for the practice area without one of the best coaches in the world stuck to their side or without a controlled strategy in place? Not very often. So if you don't have the spending power to buy this luxury then the controls that I have given to you will provide a more than adequate alternative. Head to the practice ground without them at your peril, it's your golf career.

Reaching your 4th Gear is a huge achievement, and after all that I have drummed into you about the importance of your controls the time has come to stretch your instincts and feelings further into your target orientated zone. The only way to do this is to head for the fairways with a controlled strategy in place to draw your **Signature Swing** further out of its shell into the big wide world. You don't want to be known as the "King of the Range" and the "Prince of Nothing Worth Talking About" as soon as you flop on the fairways.

You deserve to be able to stop making excuses to your golfing buddies as they try and drag you out to play on a beautiful Sunday, you have enough under your belt to hold your own. I know that the majority of you will anyway, so I may as well give you the all clear and at the same time something to hold on to. I want you to be on high alert during the big jump when moving away from the safety net of your controls. This is often initially very over-powering and should be done gradually throughout your whole building process all the way up to your **Top Gear**. **A word of warning;** use your controls on the driving range for every single shot that you play. This is the biggest mistake that the majority of club golfers make, don't fall into the same trap as the rest chasing the big cheese. Beating ball after ball into the middle of no man's land will beat your swing up black and blue. You'll finish up punch drunk, right back to square one.

In a friendly match don't be embarrassed to place your controls down and if you feel really cheeky ask if you can use a tee for a while to make sure your body maintains its well centred position. It might tickle your peers until they begin to see the results that the strategy of practising within a controlled environment can really achieve; you never know you might even start a trend. In fact you will start a trend, when they see how much you are improving they'll want to know all about it. You know where to find me…

If you're on your own use your controls for every shot that you play, gradually becoming more familiar with your swing and adapting to the challenges that the golf course presents you with. Diving in head first is the best way to crack your head open unless you know how deep the water is. Take your time; don't let anyone rush you through your building process. Your **Signature Swing** should be built at your own pace. Please don't cheat yourself out of success by telling yourself bare faced lies, wait for your instincts and feelings to give you the nod before you throw yourself into your next challenge.

Throughout the building process you are aiming for a relaxed, smooth momentum promoting a greater awareness of your body movements within your **Signature Swing**. The ball is your best teacher and be warned, without a target you have nothing to learn. Beating yourself up by over stretching yourself; lunging for the dizzy heights of your **Top Gear** too soon will unnecessarily end in tears. If you had envisaged that the building process would be whipped up in a flash then you have been misguided, great things come to those who don't wait around all day thinking about it, but gradually chip away.

Amongst all of the positive results you will be rewarded with throughout the building process there will be hiccups from time to time. You are man not machine so take a deep breath as I can reassure you that this is a natural part of the process of learning anything. If you thought you could have your cake and eat it then you had better buy some rose-tinted glasses to rest on the end of your own nose. The techniques that I have armed you with will work fantastically well in the real world and are not a pipe dream. If you follow my lead you can propel your golf as far as you are willing to take it. You need to be patient and practise in a controlled environment. You don't need to go mad and spend every waking hour doing this but it should be a gradual, regular building process, challenged by your next goal.

Your **Signature Swing** is like a flower. You firstly plant it in a sun-kissed hot spot in the best soil you have available. You water it at regular intervals but not overly or you'll drown it. As it grows you support it until it can stand on its own two feet. The support stays fixed firmly in place as its starts to blossom. When it's fully grown, smiling back at the sun, the roots are strong enough to take its weight. The stem has a solid back bone to support the full bloom of the master piece that you pumped life into with your own two hands. There is something to be said for flower power.

To trust your golf, place it into the hands of a PGA Professional

Signature Swing: 4th Gear; Personality

The 4th Gear phase of your **Signature Swing** building process is no different to the last three and is basically an extension of what you have done already. Your **Signature Swing** has started to take shape and has matured, instinctively firing from feeling, directly at your target. All great golf swings are built dynamically and look very similar throughout the initial phases up to the 3rd Gear and half swing position. This is when all great golf swings come to life; no two great swings are identical from 3rd Gear to full, as their personality develops from here, blending together with their personal framework (body) they are working within.

Please don't try to be someone you are not, you have got what you were given, if you're unhappy with your lot then you have to work on what you've got, I will show you later how effective simple preparation can be. No two golf swings are the same; we are all individually built so our own styles and personalities should never be suppressed. On the contrary you are about to make a bold statement in your quest to blow the socks clean off your golf career by creating your own master piece. Your personality is about to shine through in everything that you do as your **Signature Swing** matures, lavishing itself in feeling and instinct until you can truly call it your own.

Throughout the building process thus far you will have already got to know yourself and what fits well in your hands or you wouldn't have made it up to 3rd Gear. You may find that your rhythm is fast which suits your style of play and feels natural. I know that "slow down" is often heard on first tees all over the world but so is a lot of other helpless guidance.

Signature Swing: 4th Gear

You have probably already been plagued by the guy looking through the rose-tinted glasses forcing you to work against your natural built in tempo. Your **Signature Swing** is all about you my friend, nobody else has the right to stick their nose in and give their two-penneth worth, even if it's meant in good faith as is often the case. As your **Signature Swing** develops and matures so will the personality of your swing with your style of play. What is fast and frantic to one man is slow and rigid to another. Find what works best in your hands and your **Signature Swing** will come running to you like a child to his mother after his first day at play school.

You may feel quite vulnerable at this stage in the proceedings and your shift from 3rd to 4th Gear leaves the door wide open for the guy with the rose-tinted glasses to once again sink his teeth into your golf swing. He'll kindly point out that your little finger should be slightly further to the right or was it left and that your shoulders and hips don't quite look as they should. He knows how to press all of the right buttons to unsettle and unpick all of your progress in a vain effort to look like the *"expert"* and to get into your head.

If he was in your shoes he'd simply turn his shoulders ninety degrees, his hips forty-five degrees and keep his left arm perfectly straight to complete his backswing... He'd start his downswing with his hips and pull down with his left hand. His head would stay down and behind the ball then he'd simply turn and finish facing his target. Easy! You are an easy target right now for a little expert to put a spanner in the works. He is not you and will never be good enough to be you because little knowledge is dangerous and you already have a lot more under your belt than him to build your golf swing. I am telling you this for your own good, listening to someone that has got his head stuck in a book of facts and figures which don't add up in the real world will destroy all of your hard earned progress. The 4th Gear phase of your building process is where you might be tempted to swing over to the dark side of over-analysis and follow his lead. He's right if you want to learn from a text book dug up from the bottom of his cellar, or from the latest fad to hit the shelves. I'd rather you built your swing on your own instinct and feeling until your body finds your swing for you, pushing you to your natural limits.

The Swing killer

Over-analysis causes a hypnotic-like state forcing your third eye to wander and start to see things that are not even there or that are totally insignificant in the success or building process of your **Signature Swing**. It is easy to fall into the trap of comparison and over- analysis, often misinterpreting your own individual idiosyncrasies for a fault or short fall in your physique or technique.

A video camera in the right hands is a great tool which can monitor your progress and keep you on the straight and narrow. However, when you look with your nose pressed to the screen you start to see a new world full of angles, degrees and rotations that you weren't aware of before. I have personally had my fingers burnt big time by this one and I would highly recommend that you leave the scientific equations for the mathematicians of this world, the ones with the wooden golf swings. Unless your swing and physical conditioning programme resembles that of the best players in the world, then putting yourself up there on a split screen with Tiger or one of the gang to compare your swing ethics is just digging the hole deeper for your golf career to topple into. If you are a beginner, a high handicapper or even a reasonable club player you can liken this to running a marathon in a pair of wellington boots, not much use unless it pours down and you won't see the finishing line through the fog of confusion. One man's muck is another man's gold.

A mirror is a great way to keep your eye on your progress. These days a mirror is a standard fixture and fitting on a driving range wall that can give you instant feedback if you know where to look. A mirror won't charge you unless you break it and it won't give you a load of lip, hot enough to shoot steam out of your ears. A mirror is also less focused on the heavy technical stuff that a video screen burns into your brain. It can be a good tool in the learning process to complement your instinct and feeling, when used correctly. It is also much easier to work towards your target only orientated zone from the information and guidance a mirror gives you rather than the blunt technical details that a video camera offers, especially when working alone on your swing.

The top and bottom of it is that for the majority of the time, analysis of anything we do in life, in order to better ourselves, has a positive outcome. Cross the line into the busy road of over-analysis and your world becomes an oasis of confusion, knocking you clean off your feet. Golf is an explosive, target orientated sport that thrives off instinct and feeling. Pumping it full of technical analysis (as I know from experience) prises the gear-stick out of your hands and leaves you feeling numb and clueless, bracing yourself to crash and burn. A video camera is great to perfect the fine details but striving for perfection will get you into a head lock that will squeeze the life out of your swing, until you have no personality left to even crack a smile with. It's a fine line, you have been warned.

Signature Golf Swing: Stop fighting with complicated swing mechanics!

To trust your golf, place it into the hands of a PGA Professional

Signature Swing: 4th Gear; Up to full

You are ready to fuel your fire with the building blocks that will turn you into a raging inferno, burning your competition to a crisp. Sorry about that, what I really mean to say is that even if you are only a pussy cat dreaming of becoming a Tiger, a Tiger might be a little out of reach right now but I am going to pack your mouth full of razor sharp teeth and sharpen your claws, you'll do more than hold your own. You are ready to pack on the muscle and beef up your swing all the way to the top. Again this whole process should be a gradual learning experience, programming your body with new information and building on what you have already mastered. Your gear shift from 3rd to 4th will be smooth, clean and controlled with no hesitation or flying off the edge of the cliff before your wings are strong enough to take your weight. Give yourself time to adjust, great things come to those who act but remain patient enough to fully appreciate the fruits of their labour. Bravado and complacency are the hall marks of a fool trying to look cool.

Your 3rd Gear is feeling great, firing instinctively at your target. Your **Signature Swing** feels mature enough to move on and up in the world. You have completed the complicated bulk of the job and your base and foundations are strong enough to take the strain of anything that is thrown at you. Your first part of your **Signature Swing** up to your 3rd Gear has been built to mirror the majority of all great golf swings, it is now that you will put the icing on the cake and let your personality shine through.

As you move through your 4th Gear you are simply building an extension onto your 3rd Gear. There is nothing extravagant going on here; it is basically just more of the same until your reach the top (full swing) of your swing and your physical limitations. One thing is for sure, you will get the most out of what you have got instead, as most golfers do, of spending an entire golfing career fighting with Mother Nature which I can promise you always ends in tears. A massive factor in your learning process is being honest with yourself, identifying your limitations and working within them. If you're still not happy with your lot then it's time to work on what you've got, it's as simple as that.

Mirror image

Before you fill your baskets to the brim with balls, shaking with anticipation, eager to take the bull by the horns and rise to your next challenge you have got to work on your Mirror Image. A great way to get a feel for things and keep an eye on your progress without filling your head full of mathematical equations is to use a mirror.

Your half swing 3rd Gear as we have established has been built. As you progress with your **Signature Swing** you will feel it slowly mature as you find your feet and your body gets to grips with the additional movements. It is not a jump into 4th Gear; you will be working firstly from a half swing to a three-quarter swing, building your backswing length to mirror image that of your forward swing. Building your swing up to full is much more productive if both sides of your swing are built at the same pace, encouraging superior co-ordination, balance and control. If your backswing length is three-quarters then your forward swing should also be three quarters in length. If one side is heavier than the other then your ship could tip, topple and sink to the bottom of the ocean with all the other wrecks.

To enhance your feeling for the momentum and motion of your longer swing you could try using free flowing practice swings rolling smoothly into one another. If this is not your cup of tea then the normal stop/start practice swings starting at address and ending naturally at the finish position as in a normal playing scenario are fine. Ideally a mixture of the two styles is the most effective way to move you through your 4th Gear, but again it's a personal choice and this **Signature Swing** belongs to you my friend, you're the boss.

- Set your controls and guides in place so that you are face on to a mirror
- Take your dynamic address position within your controls
- Lift your chin, leaving your body down in your address position so that you can clearly watch your body movements
- Start the motion of your Signature Swing, aiming for 3rd Gear (waist height)
- Gradually start to increase the length of your backswing and forward swing at the same pace
- Your swing should be an extension of 3rd Gear and an extension of your guides and controls as you take it all the way up to the top

www.golfswingzone.com

Signature Swing: 4th Gear

Correct address position and early backswing take away

The club head positioned correctly below the base of the neck at waist height. The butt end of the grip points to the ball as the swing progresses, ensuring that the backswing is on plane.

Maintaining the straight left wrist which was set at address up to the top of the backswing, ensuring that the club face remains square throughout

Correctly following the guide club pointing to the right of the target with a downswing which begins slightly more inside (flatter than) that of the backswing

Following the guide (for as long as physically possible) to finish the swing well balanced and fully rotated onto the left leg, supported by the toes of the right foot

Correct address position with the left arm and left wrist as an extension of the golf club shaft. Maintaining the relationship of the left arm and club shaft as the weight begins to transfer onto the right foot to ensure that the left wrist doesn't break down

www.golfswingzone.com

Signature Golf Swing: Stop fighting with complicated swing mechanics!

The extension of the left arm and club shaft ensuring a wide swing arc as the club head is placed into the goalkeepers hands. The body weight gradually moving further onto the right foot, naturally increasing the rotation of the upper body

The left shoulder meeting the weight line which runs from inside of the right heel up through the right shoulder as the top of the backswing is reached

The body weight moving onto the left foot during the transition from backswing to downswing with the change in direction causing the wrists to give.

The stored energy contained in the wrists released as a whipping motion through impact. Continual transference of body weight onto the left side with maintenance of neutral head position with a well balanced finish on the left leg hitting the weight line that runs up from inside the left heel through the left shoulder with the right shoulder

Key points of focus:

Straight left wrist as an extension of your club shaft

The safest way to ensure that your clubface is squarely aligned throughout your backswing, reaching the top to finish square, is to maintain your firm straight left wrist set at address by your grip and take it all the way up to the top this way. Simple but very effective, very over-looked and often heavily complicated by the guy with the rose-tinted glasses. If your left wrist breaks down, so do many other of the angles and movements that naturally occur in a golf swing. If your clubface is not squarely aligned in relation to your ball and target it will have a domino effect running through and destroying every piece of the jigsaw one by one, leaving you puzzled to say the least.

If this one falls they all fall. You will have to dance around with your body in an attempt to throw compensation after compensation at your massively inconsistent golf swing. Maintain your straight, firm left wrist and the most important element of a golf swing will be guaranteed by a gold stamp at quality control. As you move up to 5th Gear later and introduce the Power in Transition your wrist action will flow from backswing into forward swing much more feely, so don't dwell on this during your 4th Gear phase

Signature Swing: 4th Gear

Starting and finishing the backswing with a straight left wrist
ensuring that the clubface remains square throughout

Centre of gravity

The moment you allow your swing to work outside of your centre of gravity it will have a profound effect on the consistency and quality of your golf shots. This is identical to how your head reacts during tennis, football or when you throw a ball. If your head, for example, is too far behind your body there will be a substantial loss of power as your body weight is forced back, restricting your rotation and weight transference. It also results in a number of inconsistent compensations in a fight or flight effort to gain control and balance. To say the outcome is erratic is an understatement.

A downswing with the head too far behind the body at impact and follow-through
restricting the weight transference and rotation

A correct and well balanced downswing and follow through

Signature Golf Swing: Stop fighting with complicated swing mechanics!

Your head should do nothing special other than to sit proudly on top of your shoulders as was intended. As you increase the length of your swing you will feel your head naturally move more in a side to side motion in compliance with your weight transference. Your body should remain well centred and well balanced throughout your swing. As you swing past impact allow your head to turn with your upper body to face the direction of your target to further promote a smooth transition from downswing to follow through.

Swing direction

Your swing direction will continue as an extension of your controls and the 3rd Gear phase of your **Signature Swing**. You will feel your hands and arms move behind your body in your backswing, in turn guiding your core rotation all the way to completion. A great way to check your position at the top of your backswing is to stand side on to a mirror. Simply take your club to the top to complete your backswing and stop. The two main check points are swing plane and clubface alignment. At the top of the backswing position your hands and club shaft should be slightly outside of your right shoulder. Your clubface should run parallel to your left forearm and your left wrist should be in the straight position that you set at address.

A correct backswing direction as an extension of the controls finishing with the hands slightly outside of the right shoulder and the clubface parallel to the left forearm

The core rotation gradually increasing up to full as a result of the combination of the weight transferring onto the right foot and the swing direction, as the backswing is completed. The left shoulder meeting the weight line which runs from the inside of the right heel up through the right shoulder

A word of warning; don't stand there all day looking for an extra degree or two, beating yourself up with doubt and disillusion. This was me at one time and is coming from the horse's mouth. It will blow your brains out leaving nothing but a cloud of smoke, a nervous twitch in your left eye and a crooked neck, so don't even go there. You should use technical details as a guide suitable for every shape, style and personality to aim for and thankfully we are all unique. That's what makes you so special, learn to love yourself first and the game of golf will love you back.

In your forward swing follow your guide line for as long as is physically possible until your hands and arms are forced to swing around your body to naturally complete the rotation of your swing. Your hands and arms will finish in a position over your left shoulder and your club shaft will run down behind your body. Your guides and controls are your safety net and if the boss of your swing is well directed everything else will follow suit. Your boss is your boss for a reason; your boss should be strong, decisive and straight to the point. If he's not kick him out and find a more superior one to take his shoes.

Signature Swing: 4th Gear

A well balanced finish with body weight over the left leg after following the guides and controls until the swing is complete

Weight transference and core rotation

These two components of your **Signature Swing** go hand in hand; one without the other is a lost cause. In your backswing gradually increase your load onto your right foot in compliance with the length of your swing. Your foot should be well planted and balanced with your weight evenly distributed. The best way to wreck all of your hard work is to start rocking and rolling all over the place in an effort to imitate Elvis, there is only one King of Rock and Roll you're not him so get over it, nobody likes a fake.

Your swing direction and weight transference work as a team, guiding your core rotation until you reach your natural limitations. If you are of reasonable flexibility your left shoulder will meet your weight line running from inside your right heel up through your right shoulder. Your left shoulder should now be tucked under your chin. Wait for your shoulder to come to your chin, if your body doesn't allow this to happen then fine, you have found your body's limitations in the rotation of your backswing. Do not forfeit your body's natural centre of gravity or weight lines trying to artificially achieve a greater rotation.

The swing direction and weight transference working as a team, guiding the core rotation until the body's natural limitations have been reached

As you begin your forward swing encourage your weight transference to flow across onto your left foot and allow the momentum created by your hand and arm swing to pull your body through impact. Let your follow through go, don't restrict its movement, let it flow using the energy and momentum created within your downswing to carry you through as far as is possible.

As you near the end of your swing your right shoulder will hit your weight line that runs up from inside of your left heel through your left shoulder. You will finish balanced with the majority of your body weight loaded on your left foot supported by the toes of your rotated right foot. Your upper body will finish its rotation facing your target.

Signature Golf Swing: Stop fighting with complicated swing mechanics!

Following the guides to completion of the swing

In **Posture: Alive and kicking, 1st Gear: Backswing and core rotation** achieving a dynamic and well balanced body in your golf swing is highly dependent upon the relationship between the centre of gravity of your body (the base of your spine) and the centre of gravity of your swing (the base of your neck).

The two points of centre of gravity which were automatically set at address by the *drop*, remaining in harmonic balance from start to finish

Throughout your **Signature Swing** it is essential that these two points of centre of gravity that were automatically set at address by the *drop*, remain in harmonic balance. If, at any given point during your swing, their relationship changes then it will directly affect the positioning of your spine angle either lifting your upper body back up out of the shot or forcing you to arch your back, both scenarios resulting in a blocked body rotation. The full significance of the important role that this plays in the effectiveness of your **Signature Swing** will be fully explained soon on your way up to **Top Gear** in **Core Rotation**

Ultimate goal

You are aiming to program your muscles with the correct swing patterns, building your swing evenly and well balanced throughout. Don't just try and get this bit out of the way as fast as possible in order to get on the driving range. You should immerse yourself in your **Signature Swing** and learn to feel how your body reacts to the new impulses running through it. Step inside of your swing and close your eyes if it helps to enhance your feeling and instincts as you gain greater control of the new you.

Picture yourself swinging to your target or always have a target in mind to guide your new swing feelings, after all without a target you have nothing to learn. Once your feelings have matured and the new technical influences are under control and becoming naturally ingrained into your flesh and bones you are setting your **Signature Swing** up for a pleasant surprise. Your *Mirror Image* is a great ice breaker for you to move more rapidly over to your exclusive target orientated zone when you take it to the driving range. Don't expect miracles but I'm sure it will bring a smile to your

Signature Swing: 4th Gear

face much faster than without firstly perfecting your Mirror Image. Skip this stage and you are missing out on something special.

Take it onto the driving range

This is the moment you have been waiting for to get the bit between your teeth and find out what it's all about. This is not the time for the hero in you to swagger out into the sunset pulling his horse and bag of dynamite behind him. When your **Signature Swing** is successfully fully built, distance will never be an issue again. Fall at this hurdle through a shortfall in patience and self-control and you will forfeit the game, dealing yourself a hand full of jokers. Smooth consistency are the hall marks of a great golf swing no different to a great pint of Guinness; pull it too fast and it's drinkable but lacking in quality and you just can't put your finger on why. You know your **Signature Swing** well enough by now to tune your own individual speed of play to the new movements for maximum results throughout your development; I just thought I'd run it past you one more time.

To trust your golf, place it into the hands of a PGA Professional

True impact up to top gear

- Focus on your target
- Focus on your ball
- React to your target (hit the ball)

Here we go again I hear you say, well if it's the secret great players have known for generations then it's good enough for us. This is the moment that you pump instinctive feeling straight into the heart of your 4th Gear phase as you gradually increase the length of your **Signature Swing** up to full. You have already mastered the ground work, perfecting your Mirror Image. All you need to do at this stage is to select a target, grab a bucket of balls and throw as many instinctive impulses at your target as your grey matter can handle. Allow your instinct, rhythm and feeling to let their hair down and run wild.

You have already gelled your **Signature Swing** up to 4th Gear in front of the mirror. To be honest that's as difficult as it gets, never the less I will leave nothing to chance and will break down the procedure so that you have a strategy on the driving range that you can repeat with each shot that you play. You are standing on the driving range with all of your controls in place; make sure you do because I'm watching you…

You have built the 3rd Gear phase of your **Signature Swing**. It feels natural and is firing instinctively at your target. This is where you put your top hat on and get the show on the road all the way to the top. Please build on top of your 1st, 2nd and 3rd Gear foundations with the following:

Signature Swing: 4th Gear all the way up to the top

- Begin practice swinging with your eyes firmly fixed on your target

Signature Golf Swing: Stop fighting with complicated swing mechanics!

- Address your ball dynamically, ready to fire into action with your feet just under shoulder width apart
- Turn only your head and focus once again on your target

- Turn your head back to your ball and focus on your ball
- Your target is the only thought in your mind's eye

- Let your swing go and react to your target
- Swing back and push the guide ball away or swing over your guide tee without spoiling the party by hitting your single malt. As you do, transfer your body weight smoothly onto your right foot

Signature Swing: 4th Gear

- Maintain your straight left wrist and the extension of your club shaft with your left hand and arm at all times. Place your club head into the goalkeeper's hands, he's waiting for it. Feel your body weight loaded but light on your right foot

- Continue swinging back on the line of your controls. You will feel your hand and arm swing, naturally increasing your core rotation as they move behind your body

- Maintain your firm, straight left wrist all the way to the top of your backswing, to guarantee that your clubface is square, ready to begin your downswing. Your clubface will be parallel to your left forearm at the top of your backswing

- As you reach the top of your backswing your left shoulder will meet the weight line running from inside your right heel up through your right shoulder. If your flexibility allows it your left shoulder should fit neatly under your chin

- At the top of your backswing your hands are slightly outside of your right shoulder with your left arm in a straight position and your right arm folded neatly at the elbow around your body. Your left arm does not need to be perfectly straight so if it isn't, don't beat yourself up over it. You are not alone; just take a look at some of the great players on Tour!

- At the top of your backswing your club shaft should ideally be parallel to the ball to target line. If it's not don't beat yourself up. There are many great players walking the fairways with an across the line (pointing to the right of the target) or laid off (pointing to the left of the target) position at the top of the backswing. Your main concern is a square clubface throughout and to finish at the top of your backswing. Your style of swing is in your hands; don't fight with your **Signature**.

Signature Golf Swing: Stop fighting with complicated swing mechanics!

- Swing down on the line of your guide club slightly to the right of your target, incorporating your release and smoothly transfer your body weight across on to your left foot. The transition from backswing to forward swing should be synchronised without any one dominant movement taking the lead

- As you continue down through the impact area and into your follow through your weight shifts further onto your left foot. Your release is working as one with your swing direction presenting a square clubface in relation to your target at impact and shortly thereafter

Signature Swing: 4th Gear

- Allow your head to turn with your body into your follow through just after your impact position, to finish looking in the direction of your target

- Into your follow through and beyond make sure that your follow through single malt is still standing tall. The momentum and direction of your swing will guide the natural rotation of your body, finishing with the majority of your body weight firmly planted on your left foot. Allow your right foot to naturally turn to support your rotation and weight shift by finishing balanced up onto your toes
- The rotation of your upper body will be completed by your right shoulder meeting the weight line running from inside of your left heel and up through your left shoulder
- Your hands and arms swing over your left shoulder and your club shaft comes to rest behind your body
- You have finished your swing well balanced on your left foot with your chest facing your target and your head ideally placed over your body, looking in the direction of your target

Your **Signature Swing** is successfully built, standing proud. If your 3rd Gear is solidly built then your 4th Gear will be a formality. The whole building process to complete your 4th Gear revolves around your target; remember that without it you have nothing to learn. As you have already experienced, practising within a controlled environment is the most productive. This saves you a lot of wasted time and energy, making every moment that you spend on the driving range count. With a little elbow grease all four gears of your **Signature Swing** will be instinctively reacting to your target, a job well done! Give yourself a big pat on the back; you're another step closer to your **Top Gear**.

To trust your golf, place it into the hands of a PGA Professional

Signature Swing: 5th Gear

Signature Swing: 5th Gear; Power in transition

Your **Signature Swing** has matured, full bodied, firing instinctively at your target. The time has come for you to realise the true Power in Transition, to maximise and fully utilise the dynamics of your **Signature Swing**. Before you do anything be sure that you have fully understood **The Power in Transition** explained earlier.

Feel the power of transition

- Grip your golf club correctly from the one o'clock position
- Hold your hands out in front of your body

- Swing your golf club at just above waist height around your body as you would with a baseball swing
- With firm, tension free wrists gradually increase the speed of this swing
- As you begin the forward swing you will now feel your wrists give, due to the change in direction

Above is the exercise that was covered earlier to help you understand how the transition from backswing to forward swing naturally forces your wrists to break, unleashing the whipping motion that produces the power. Before you run off to the driving range with a hand full of your most lethal weapons I insist that you take a step back in order to make a massive leap into the very near future.

The transition phase is just like a wild stallion that has never been mounted before. Throw a saddle on without firstly getting to know him and you'll be bucked straight off. Be sure to get up and away as fast as you hit the deck or he'll trample all over you. Take a step back on the other hand and go in slowly with a pocket full of goodies to firstly gain his

Signature Golf Swing: Stop fighting with complicated swing mechanics!

trust and with a little pampering, patience and tender loving care he'll happily let you take the reins. Sit tight and enjoy the ride; a beast will never be fully tamed but work with him, the natural force that he is and every second will be as thrilling as the last.

In **Signature Swing: 1st and 2nd Gears; Step up to the challenge** your body was taken out of play so that you could gain control over the boss of your swing, your swing direction. The first thing to buckle as you introduce the power in transition is your swing direction. This, as you are now fully aware, pulls and pushes your body around like the school-boy bully. You've hit the bully once but he's just got back up so before he gets chance to regain his composure you're going to have to hit him again, only this time twice as hard.

I can't tell you how much you will benefit by firstly taking your body out of play, introducing the Power in Transition and marrying it together with your swing direction and clubface alignment. As soon as your instincts and feelings give you the green light you can pack on the muscle and unleash the true impact that using your swing dynamics to the max can achieve. To increase the forces in transition you can place more weight at the club head end to exaggerate the feeling. This can be of great benefit initially to develop trust and to gain a greater feeling for the transition phase of your swing, but it is not a must, the choice is yours.

Aim to gradually increase the momentum as you smoothly approach your transition from backswing to forward swing with firm but relaxed hands. This will place forces onto your wrists making them give, as you change direction and swing down into your forward swing. Make sure that your swing is one continuous, smooth movement without a pause or break in momentum. The swing drill below should be performed identically to **Signature Swing: 1st and 2nd Gears; Step up to the challenge** with added emphasis on the **Power in Transition.**

Standing within your guides and controls and with firm but relaxed hands:

- Begin practice swinging with your eyes firmly fixed on your target

- Address your ball dynamically, ready to fire into action, with your feet together
- Turn your head only and focus once again on your target. Then Turn your head back to your ball and focus on your ball. Your target is the only thought in your mind's eye

Signature Swing: 5th Gear

- Let your swing go and react to your target
- Swing back and push the guide ball away or swing over your guide tee, without spoiling the party by hitting your single malt

- Maintain your straight left wrist and the extension of your club shaft with your left hand and arm at all times.

- Place your club head into the goalkeeper's hands, he's waiting for it

- Swing down on the line of your guide club slightly to the right of your target, missing your other single malt and unleash your release to fire squarely. Smack your target straight between the eyes

Signature Golf Swing: Stop fighting with complicated swing mechanics!

Initially it will be difficult to find and to time the feeling for the transition. You may feel as though you are losing some control over your club head through impact which is one of the main reasons I wanted you to start without your body. Once the acceleration and change in direction leads smoothly into your downswing you will begin to feel your club head lag slightly. The power from this lag is then released at impact in a whipping motion from your wrists.

The whipping motion created by the transition generates a substantial gain in momentum and club head speed resulting in increased power which translates into distance. Another great benefit is a sharper (steeper) angle of attack, resulting in cleaner and far superior ball striking. This is one of the reasons good players astonish less experienced golfers by often taking big, deep divots, firstly striking the ball then the ground. I'm afraid that vice-versa is the hallmark of the classic chopper often suffering from a swing plane problem that can only dream about back spin. You will never be (or are no longer) that guy, you'll need a bulldozer to repair your pitch marks from now on as your ball grips and rips the green to shreds.

To trust your golf, place it into the hands of a PGA Professional

Pack on the muscle: Power in transition

As your instincts and feelings mature and you are happy with your progress you can begin to pack on the muscle. The easiest way to introduce the Power in Transition is to firstly work from your 3rd Gear half swing gradually building up to your 4th Gear full swing. The introduction of your body can initially prove to be quite tricky, adding a new dimension which includes more rotations and movements. The secret lies in gaining superior control over your weight transference and rotation with the guidance of your swing direction to unleash the power in transition.

It is the transition from backswing to forward swing that produces the whipping motion; therefore the change in direction and shift in your body weight from right foot to left foot is the key to mastering this during the transition. The transition phase should flow; one thing that really helped me was to feel as though there was no end to the movement, my backswing flows into my downswing and my downswing doesn't give my backswing chance to pause. Imagine your forward swing as a continuation of your backswing, the angle and club head lag will naturally be produced by the change in direction, forcing your firm but tension free wrists to give. As a great player completes his backswing he will often describe the feeling of a pause or delay in the motion. This is created by the angle of lag that the club head produces as it briefly moves closer to the body as your wrists give and the angle of lag is increased. Eventually your club head will have to be redirected into the downswing to follow your hands and arms until the stored energy can no longer be contained within your downswing. It then shoots to the furthest point away from your core; your hands. The energy created forces your wrists to act within a powerful whipping motion, propelling your club head towards your ball with great power, weight and speed. This is the reason that a slightly built golfer can still hit the ball a great distance by utilising the full dynamics of his swing to the max.

To truly master the Power in Transition your **Signature Swing** will become one movement, with your backswing and forward swing flowing into one another. The only true way to utilise the dynamics of your golf swing is to use the Power in Transition and the change in direction that creates it. If you pause at the top of your backswing the power that lies within the motion is removed to leave only the bare bones behind. If you work together hand in hand with Mother

Nature the rewards are guaranteed to be dynamic. Your Signature Swing has reached its 5th Gear and it's in one piece. Standing within your controls and guides with firm but relaxed hands please proceed as follows:

- As you complete your backswing your rotation meets your weight line (your left shoulder hits the weight line running from the inside of your right heel up through your right shoulder). At this point be prepared to continue the motion into your downswing, allowing no time for a break or pause to interrupt your natural momentum

- Use the Power in Transition contained in the change in direction as your body weight begins to move across onto your left foot. You will feel your wrists having no other option than to give, creating a split second lag often referred to by great players as a delay or pause "at the top"

- As you continue into your downswing the lag and angle of wrist hinge will open up at a given point due to the momentum, making it impossible to contain. This creates a whipping like motion and sensation firing directly through your ball

Signature Golf Swing: Stop fighting with complicated swing mechanics!

- Continue through impact to finish your swing bigger, better and stronger than ever before

- Your entire Power in Transition revolves around your target. Without a target you have nothing to learn. Embrace your instinctive feeling and your Signature Swing will embrace the moment whole-heartedly and your talent will shine through

Welcome to The Power in transition. Your 5th Gear is on the highway to Top Gear.
To trust your golf, place it into the hands of a PGA Professional

Top Gear

- Focus on your target
- Focus on your ball
- React to your target (hit the ball)

Your **Top Gear** can only truly fully fire on all cylinders when you are solely in your target orientated zone. For you to be in your **Top Gear** your swing mechanics have to belong to the guy behind the wheel who is in total control. If he's not and his swing is scattered out on a cold hard floor covered in oil waiting for all of the nuts, bolts and body parts to be screwed on to the main chassis then his **Top Gear** will be jammed in 1st Gear, revving its backside off.

I totally understand that building your **Signature Swing** is a process that takes time to pump instinct and feeling into. The majority of you have already taken to the fairways and have already discovered that it is not all plain sailing on the way up to your **Top Gear**. Success is never done and dusted in five minutes. I agree that there are people walking this planet with pure raw talent but a champion doesn't just fall from the sky.

I can guarantee that a major contributing factor in your level of satisfaction and achievement will be playing to a controlled strategy which is, as often as possible, within a controlled environment. Regular, focused practice is the only way to reinforce the correct patterns of muscle memory which eventually take the physical movement out of the gap between your ears and place it into your hands. How do you ride a bike? How do you throw a ball? How do you catch a ball? How do you kick a ball? The list of physical movements that you have previously ingrained into the hard drive deep within your muscles is endless. By taking the emphasis away and off your grey matter your body can work on auto-pilot, performing the physical task in question in a completely different mode. This is something that you will learn in more detail shortly in **The Zone**.

This is how you know that you have truly reached your **Top Gear**. Your swing mechanics have been repeatedly drilled into your bones each time you have played. This type of consistent practice programs your muscles to take the strain off your brain and all of the heavy technical thought patterns that come with over-analysis. The old saying "it's like riding a bike" rings true for many of the day-to-day physical movements that we perform without thinking twice. Before you start, your age or physical stature don't stand up in an argument or as an excuse. Yes it would be more rewarding and a faster more productive process if you were in your prime, I'd be lying if I didn't agree, but an old dog can learn new tricks so stop making excuses. You can be so much better, you know it's true, so just do it. If you are young and in your prime I am arming you with information that I wish I knew when I first held a golf club in my hands. The golfing world is now your oyster.

If you have never ridden a bike before, yes it might take a little longer than a determined five year old that doesn't understand the fear factor and complicated thought process that wants to know the ins and outs of everything running through an adult brain. The end result will be the same, however, if your learning process is regular, focused and as determined as the steely glare that the five year old has every morning when he sees his bike in the corner of his father's shed. Stabilisers are for wimps he shouts, stamping his feet but you know they will support him and protect him from the pain of defeat and falling face down in a puddle of doubt and despair. You know his day will come as he matures and his confidence grows to go it alone. You rightfully do what's best for your child and his development in this sometimes cruel world so that he can grow to stand proudly on his own two feet and hold his own. There is a child in us all, so why neglect your own progress. Your father mounted your stabilisers for a reason.

Your target is your guiding light, without it you will be dragging your heels and waving your hands and arms around in an attempt to find your way out of the darkness. With no target you have nothing to learn and will never know how great (or dismal) you are. Your ball is your best teacher. Watch it's every move and learn to love the feedback that it throws at you; you have enough ammunition in reserves to come back with all guns blazing.

Your controls represent me as I guide you through your learning process. Your guides will make sure that the time you spend on your golf is time well spent. Whatever your standard, if you don't have a controlled strategy, set up within a controlled environment, then the little devil in us all has time to work his way into your life. Your swing is like a sponge; it soaks up every drop of wisdom you feed it with. Your controls and guides are your back bone. Without them the chances that your swing will fall to bits is out of my hands and yours; you're on your own, may luck cross your path.

The golf course is a completely different animal to the driving range mirror; if you go in unprepared it will chew you up and spit you out. If you firstly take to the fairways and use your controls you can adjust and work your **Signature Swing** into the change of environment to tame the jungle animal that a golf course can be. This also keeps your mind's eye focused on your target and reacting to it because you feel reassured that your **Signature Swing** is under control. As your feelings and instincts mature and start to give you the green light you can contemplate removing your controls whilst on the fairways. You can then work exclusively in your target orientated zone with a honed and finely tuned natural, instinctive golf swing. When things go wrong you don't need to run off to find a shoulder to cry on, you have a strategy in place that you can call on as and when required, to put you back on the straight and narrow.

If it was down to me, every time you went to play this game called golf that you love so much you would firstly stand on the driving range and smoothly work through your gears until you hit **Top Gear**. Yes that's right, you would start in 1st Gear and smoothly, one by one, shift through to reach **Top Gear**. Imagine starting your car first thing in the morning and putting your gear stick straight into **Top Gear**, your car wouldn't get off your driveway never mind get you to work on time. It would splutter and stall. If you treat your **Signature Swing** with the same lack of compassion you are setting yourself up for a massive back-fire that won't look cool when you've got jump leads wrapped around your neck. You'll be left standing in a cloud of hot air making excuses like, "it's not normally this bad…I don't know what went wrong today… I played great last week on my own in my greenhouse swinging between the tomatoes and spring onions in front of the tooth fairy…"

The only person you are cheating out of a **Signature Swing** that is solidly built to perform with instinct and feeling running through its veins is yourself. You no longer need the help of the guy with the rose-tinted glasses propped on the end of his nose; bite your tongue and let his running commentary go in one ear and out of the other. If the commentary is persistently and annoyingly poor run a four minute mile in the opposite direction every time he shows his face. Eventually he'll get the message.

As I promised you at the very beginning there is absolutely no reason why you can't do this on your own with a little elbow grease and the hands of the most important golfer in your world, you of course. As your **Signature Swing** develops stay true to yourself and learn from every drop of feedback your ball throws at you. **Top Gear** is the place to be, your golf is now in the fast lane, firing on all cylinders and on a road to somewhere full of satisfaction and success.

Together we have made it happen. Congratulations my friend, it's more important to me than you will ever know!

To trust your golf, place it into the hands of a PGA Professional

Signature Swing: Master plan

As you gradually shift through the gears and your **Signature Swing** matures and grows you will start to develop your own dominant shape. Your dominant shape of shot (ball flight) will actually find you and is naturally born, thriving on the way that your body moves and reacts to your target. You have two options; the first is to play with it and allow your personality and style to shine through in every shot that you play. The second option is to fight with it in search of the lush, greener grass on the other side of the fence thickly carpeting your neighbours back garden.

 www.golfswingzone.com

Fighting with Mother Nature (talking from experience here) will result in you chasing your tail with no end in sight until your golf career hits a brick wall head on and hard. You'll be at best half the player you could have been with the added aggravation of being known as Sick Note; the most injury prone swinger in town.

Next time you drive your car, step on the gas with your left foot and control your clutch with your right foot and guess what? This puts you in the same predicament as your golf career. You will be at best half the driver you ever were and a danger not only to yourself but everyone else around you. Thankfully golf is not life or death but often feels like it on the 19th hole after a round of fighting with at least ten of the golf clubs in your bag and acting against your own instinctive behaviour.

If you are right-handed try and write a letter left-handed, hammer a nail into a piece of wood left-handed, play tennis or throw a ball left-handed. The fact of the matter is that you never for one moment consider going against Mother Nature in the majority of other aspects of your daily life or the sporting events that you take part in. For some unknown reason golf digs deep and presses all the right buttons that eventually spin you around in desperation leaving you believing that your only option is to grab at straws. Your **Signature Swing** is above all of this and you know that when things go wrong it can be built up again by simply running through the gears in your own time and at your own pace, with the two hands of the most important golfer in your world.

Jack Nicklaus, one of the greatest players of all time, once revealed that before a tournament he'd go to the driving range and hit some balls to find his shot for the day. Every day he would have a different shot for that day. Don't get me wrong he wasn't perfecting his Pull Hook and building a strategy to play with it on the golf course. His Power Fade is legendary and he was great enough to understand that nobody's perfect and when they are it's certainly never all of the time. He was sharp enough to know that every day brings along with it a new set of challenges that require a different mind-set and strategy to pull the best out of his top draw.

He would go to the driving range to see how much fade spin that particular day would bring, play with it and integrate it into his course strategy, shaping his mind's eye, ready for the fairways where it mattered most. He must have known that fighting with himself was the least of his worries and that it held no priority at all if he expected to beat his competitors the way that he did. The ball was his best teacher. He would watch and learn from it and feel the amount of spin that the day brought with it. His ultimate judge; his target, would throw instant feedback at him with exact measurements that he could build into his winning strategy. The man was a genius and understood that often something complicated is something simple that is not fully understood, that's why he is "The Golden Bear" and a legend in his own right.

Great players know not to dwell too long on what doesn't work but to focus on what works best for them. Often a pupil will come to me having practised finding his dominant shape to be a gentle fade. "I want a draw" Are the first words out of his mouth, if I ask why, he replies, "draw spin creates more roll, is more powerful and I'll hit the ball further." This is true but for the sake of a few metres if a fade is your natural shot and you can call upon it at the drop of a hat, why would you want to change? A fade offers greater control, your ball stops quicker on the green and the loss of distance is minimal, these are all small insignificant details. A draw has great benefits too if it is your natural, dominant shape of shot. It is all swings and roundabouts, don't fight it, go with it. The ball will be your best teacher, holding your hand through the process and eventually selecting the shot that shines the brightest for your personal **Signature Swing**.

Something that escapes most amateur golfer's minds is the fact that every great player in the world of golf feels nervous leading up to and in the crunch situations of a tournament, particularly on the finishing holes in the final round. To be a true champion requires tremendous drive and ambition which is burned into the heart of the winner who has dreamed about winning during every waking moment, tucking the dream into bed every night. A champion doesn't just appear out of thin air, the person you see crying on his knees on the final green with his head in his hands when the winning put drops has worked his whole life towards this moment, with dedication given to very few people. The glory looks great but what goes on behind the curtain demands hours of steely determination. We are all made of the same stuff but some people can handle it better than others and can push the pressure away, regaining focus to capitalise on their strengths, shooting them along the road to victory. No great player hits a ball that flies as straight as an arrow especially in a moment of pressure. They call on their reserves to find something that they can truly rely on to perform, a shot that's part of their natural make up, their dominant shape.

I am about to explain the benefits of a dominant shape and how effective a ball flight that consistently curves in one direction can be. Before we get there it might be hard for some of you to believe that there are great players walking the fairways of the world as we speak that play their whole round with a slight push aiming slightly left of their original target and pushing the ball slightly right in the direction of their target. Their style of swing, physical characteristics and instincts have chosen a push as their dominant shape that best fits their game plan. Only a fool would tamper with this, especially working up to and on the verge of the moment of glory.

Your dominant shape

The dominant shape of shot that you will develop as your **Signature Swing** matures is something you should grab with both hands and cherish. It is now that you can start to build a strategy that revolves around your **Signature Swing**, which will turn you into the master of your own mechanics. **A word of warning;** a ball flight that initially begins its flight to the left of its target is a sure fire sign that the owner has a weak swing. If you don't understand why then please go back to your **Signature Swing: 1st Gear Downswing; Let Down** and don't do anything from here until you know what you are doing.

Dominant ball flights you are striving for:

- **Fade:** Begins straight and curves gently to the right
- **Draw:** Begins straight and curves gently to the left
- **Gentle Push:** Begins slightly right and stays there

We are all made with various strengths and weaknesses and dominant traits live and breathe within us all. With a little time, patience and through well rubbed-in elbow grease your dominant shape of shot will start to shine brightly. Don't try fighting it, go with it, it has chosen your **Signature Swing** for a reason. Great players know that to be great you have got to find what works in your hands and develop a strategy around it. This is the reason that great players are great; they don't focus on the negatives and their weaknesses but instead focus on their strengths, working with them and eventually mastering them.

Master your strategy

By developing a strategy for your natural shape you will be forever armed with a treasure chest of wealth every time you set foot on the fairways. Fighting with yourself is a thing of the past. Your dominant shape will work for you so let's see how great you can be...

For this example, let's assume that your natural, dominant shot is a draw. Ideally the optimal position for your shot to finish is in the centre of the fairway.

You know that your ball will have draw spin curving to the left.

- Aim to hit your ball down the right side of the fairway and your ball will naturally produce draw spin, finishing in the centre of the fairway as planned

Golf, as we all know, doesn't always work out this way. If it did it would bore the socks off us. If your shot is not perfectly executed how can you increase the size of your landing area?

- Aim to hit your ball down the right side of the fairway. This time your ball doesn't produce any draw spin as planned but lands safely on the right side of the fairway
- Aim to hit your ball down the right side of the fairway. This time your ball produces too much draw spin but because you started your shot down the right side, the left side of the fairway safely catches your ball

Most amateur golfers don't have a dominant shot or don't have a strategy in place to use their dominant shot to its full potential. If you aim your ball straight down the middle of the fairway you will only have half of the fairway to hit (and miss) or to play with. If your dominant shot produces too much draw spin, as it will from time to time, without a sound strategy in place your ball will career cleanly over the white markers or will make a big splash into the middle of the duck pond. Take your pick...

Great players know that golf is not a game of perfection they know that they won't hit every shot perfectly. That is why they use their strengths on the golf course to the max. If your dominant shot is a draw then you know that your ball flight will move from right to left, so if you aim down the right side of the fairway, you will have the whole fairway to play with.

If you master your dominant shape and develop a strategy that fits well, your winning formula will be in place, ready to change the way that you see the fairways forever.....

To trust your golf, place it into the hands of a PGA Professional

The Zone

Great players are mentally and physically prepared to play great golf. I have heard elite sportsmen and world class athlete's talk about their Zone as a quiet place where the spectators are a wash of colours. It is a place that feels slow and controlled, even when things are getting crazy all around them. Often when someone is in their Zone they don't recall a lot of what took place around them, they are in their own world or bubble, fully in control but running on auto-pilot. It all seems to happen on its own.

A great way to relate to this, if you don't think you have ever been in your Zone is to think about something that you do in your day-to-day life, like driving to work. Have you ever arrived at your destination but didn't remember how you got there? You were in your Zone. You have learnt to drive. It wasn't easy in the beginning, there was the gear stick, peddles, mirror and of course the other drivers to think about. With time and practice all of these things automatically became second nature. You didn't need to think about the physical movements anymore because you practised the same basics over and over again. This results in you having the ability to drive in a different mode using a different part of your brain with the ultimate target of arriving safely at your desired destination. If you can't drive or are too young it is the same when you ride your bike, walk to the shop for your morning paper or throw a ball. You are in your Zone more often than you thought my friend...

In life it is easier to think about what can go wrong rather than how great things can be, this has been proven. Our brain recalls our poor performances at lightning speed. The demons are there in a flash and you've guessed it, a negatively programmed brain doesn't very often result in greatness, if ever at all.

Great players, athletes and business men fight these negative thought patterns every day. That's right; your heroes are only human and think just like the rest of us. Every highly successful person feels nervous, feels the pressure and at times (as we all do) has low self-esteem. You are not on your own. Highly successful individuals don't give up without a fight but there is more to it than that, they have a strategy in place that they practise on a regular basis which gives them the strength and composure to defeat the demons within.

We all know that to improve your physical strength you go to the gym and work out. After your first few times you don't really see too much of a difference until you find a routine that works for you, with a planned strategy built into or around your life. Over time you feel fitter and stronger and have a new lease of life. It gives you great satisfaction to see your hard work and dedication come to fruition. Don't work out for a month or two and what happens? Most of what you have built up is lost and you are back to square one but with the added advantage of knowing that it is possible and that you can get it back. Working with the computer between your ears is no different, your physical appearance and the way you hold yourself will also change. That's what confidence does to a person. You will feel sharper, more focused and more confident to reach your goals. If you stop working out with your brain muscles they also get smaller and weaker and inevitably this affects your performance at work and at play.

I don't know of any champion that just fell from the sky and landed softly on a bubble of gold and glory. You firstly need a strategy that combines both the physical and mental aspects of your goals. On the golf course this is to get your ball in the hole with the least amount of shots. The strategy must be simple yet effective and above all repeated the same way, time and time again. If you start to think about changing the gears of your car with a different hand or in a different way then you start to become a danger to the other motorists, as we have already established. You will never forget how to drive your car or ride your bike because you practise the same principles every time you go for a spin. Your muscles have stored the movement deep within their memory banks, never to be forgotten. This is what building up using the basic principles and repeating them ultimately achieves; deep ingrained muscle memory that is hard to shake. This is another reason your **Signature Swing** should be pumped and fuelled only with positive influences, instead of ingraining the negatives; you'll be shaking them off.

Being unprepared is a fatal mistake in any walk of life, from rock climbing to giving a speech. Poor preparation, especially under pressure, results in failure. Preparation is the key. If you want to play the best golf of your life you need to prepare to play the best golf of your life. It will not only propel your golf to another hemisphere but golf will be more fun than you ever imagined and not the hard slog it often can be. You firstly need a goal. It doesn't matter how big the goal is, the bigger the better as far as I'm concerned. If you shoot for the stars, then on a bad day at least you'll hit the tops of the trees which is more than most even dare. Don't be afraid, go for it. Your dream and goal must be sat in the middle of a well-planned, simple yet effective strategy that places your body and mind fully into your Zone.

You are in control, you control how you think and your mind is stronger than you ever imagined. In anything in life you have the basics. The better the basics the better you are. If you master the basics you will become a master yourself. I don't care who you are or what your goals are, the one thing that I am sure about is that you will be even more exceptional when you fire up your **Golf Swing Zone.**

Your Golf Swing Zone: Key Elements

Your Golf Swing Zone is a well-planned strategy with a simple, repeatable system which programs your brain and body in preparation for where and when it matters the most.

If you want to do something well you have to start as you mean to go on. I often see golfers fumbling around in their bag searching for the magic club with a permanent frown on their face. Being decisive is more important than the club you are holding in your hands. By all means take your time to evaluate the situation as long as it takes you to find the best weapon for the shot, but the moment that you reach into your bag, tell yourself this is the one that's going to do the best job. If you really don't trust it throw it back in your bag until you find one that you do. If indecision takes over you may as well stop there and then. Your Zone is of little help when your head is stuck in a cloud of confusion. If you get distracted and your focus is somewhere other than being in your Zone, don't hesitate. Stop and re-start the process from the very beginning. From this moment forward you have no excuses for poor preparation, if you do hit a poor shot at least at the end of the day you can hold your head high and say to yourself "I gave it my best."

There are nine key, fundamental elements that must be part of your Pre-Shot Routine for you to fully reach your **Golf Swing Zone**. Every golf shot that you play your ball is your best teacher and never forget that without a target you have nothing to learn.

1. Focus on your target
2. Visualise your shot going to the target
3. Practise swings focused on your target or with your target in mind
4. Stand to Attention
5. Focus on your target
6. Slowly inhale a deep breath
7. Focus on your ball with your target in mind
8. Slowly exhale a deep breath
9. React to your target, let your swing flow freely

1. Focus on your Target

The moment that your concentration is broken and your focus distracted, your eyes begin to wander until the blinding headlights of negativity burn a deep wound into your memory banks. A golf course is loaded with highly addictive distractions that seduce your brain and draw your focus away from your end goal. The golfer's tale of so near yet so far is legendary and bounced off club house walls all over the world. The dreaded water hazard, bunker or tight fairway that acts like a magnet and wrecks the card of the eye of the beholder every time it counts, is infamous.

If you throw a ball what is the last thing you look at before you release it? If you kick a ball what is the last thing you see before you focus on the ball to kick it? This is not rocket science and it's something that we all do in the majority of the other sports we play or in the day-to-day physical tasks we perform. If you were driving your car down a winding country road and looked into the field on the left hand side at the cattle grazing, if your focus was too long and overly intense your car would follow your lead veering left naturally, with your line of vision controlling your physical actions. Inevitably your car would head in the direction in which you are looking. You would end up sat in the middle of the field with the grazing cattle which may be quite pleasant for a while until you realise that you have no wellington boots with you, your mobile phone signal in the countryside is weak and your wheels are spinning in the cow's business. If you don't believe me, be my guest. I've heard it's lucky and you might come out smelling of roses.

You're standing on the tee of a reasonably tight par four with out of bounds down the left side and a water hazard running the whole length of the fairway's right side. The white markers are shining brightly. You remember all too well the last time you played; you were way off the mark and had to reload on the tee and take a penalty. You're stuck between the devil and the deep blue sea of a rather large water hazard on your right side. You address your ball and focus on your target, focus on your ball then look up once more and the white markers catch your line of vision, just a quick peek to see if they are still there. Your backswing feels fine then it hits you, you don't want to wreck your card like last time with an out ball, so take your pick; bottling out, panic and/or hesitation is what happens next.

Out of bounds takes over your head. You don't want to go there again so what do you do? Over compensate and fire the ball as far away as possible from your point of fear. Your ball is now making waves in the middle of the duck pond. If your last point of focus worked the way it should then your ball has finished in the direction of your last point of focus. Your ball is in the middle of the farmer's field, sat amongst the cows and clearly out of bounds. It is of no consolation even if you can see your ball; you'd literally have to take the bull by its horns to get at it. Your last point of focus would rightfully be where your ball has finished. Through lack of knowledge or if misused your last point of focus actually becomes the place that you are really trying to avoid. Reload. This type of behaviour and vague focus has a double-sided magnet effect, either drawing your ball towards your last point of focus or propelling your ball over to the other hemisphere, a million miles away from your greatest fear.

To make being in your Zone work effectively, your last point of focus must be your target. Your brain is the most advanced piece of kit that has ever been known to man. If you use it the way it was programmed and designed to work, your **Signature Swing** will never look back again. Your last point of focus is the picture that your mind's eye stores in its memory banks. With split second engineering it fires and processes its brain waves, shooting them directly into your muscles, ligaments, bones, impulses, instincts and feelings amongst many other things, like a lightning bolt. If you are pointing your brain in the wrong direction by looking in the wrong place you may as well close your eyes and hope for the best. In doing this as well as all of the other instructions, your body and brain have to put together a master plan of compensation in a fight to get you back on track, in the time it takes you to blink your eyes. Not an easy job even for a brain like yours, does all this sound familiar? It is amazing how strongly these signals condition your brain into negative thought patterns which in turn affect the way that you physically react to a given situation.

Your **Signature Swing** revolves around your target, after all golf is an explosive, target orientated sport that thrives on and is judged by how many shots it takes you to reach your target. If your target is not at the forefront of your game plan then you are leaving the door wide open for the little devil in us all to come out to play with your head. As you are fully aware you have to fill your head with your target and your target only, to truly instinctively react to it from feeling alone.

Your target is not only "King" it will be "The Only Thing" as your **Signature Swing** fully matures. If this is all getting too much for you then liken this to archery, darts, snooker or any other target orientated sport. If you have a target to aim for then why think about anything else that has the potential to put you off and make you miss? Where do you think a marksman looks when he's about to pull the trigger, at his finger? He is aiming at the smallest target or smallest point within his target because he knows that if you aim big you miss big, but if you aim small then you miss small. It's not complicated stuff but it will blow your mind when you see how effective something so simple can be in the development of your **Signature Swing**.

- Select a target that fits the shot you want to play and focus on it
- Your target should be as small as possible, to enhance your focus. This will limit the possibility of distraction and if you miss, you miss small
- If your target is distant by this I mean outside of approximately one hundred metres then pick out a small branch of a tree which is directly in line but above your intended target. If there are no trees then anything in the sky line directly above your target. The reasoning behind this is to further limit the distractions making it easier to focus
- As your target gets closer the target becomes the target, you don't need to find a substitute for a 50 meter pitch unless you can't see the green or the flag
- Without a target you have nothing to learn or aim for

Your Zone is filled with your target. Be decisive, why look at or think about anything else?

2. Visualise your shot going to the target

Your head is full with your target; your next step is to reinforce this thought process further with the power of visualisation. If you think you can do something, you are right. If you think you can't, then you haven't got a chance in a month of Sundays. As soon as you start to think about topping, hooking, a dreaded socket or whatever your weakness may be, what happens? Your hairs stand up on the back of your neck, you grip your golf club like a gorilla and your swing falls to pieces around your feet. If you believe all of this positive thinking and prancing around trying to convince yourself you're the best is beyond little old you then go and find a mirror. You are now looking back at yourself with a big frown. How does it feel? Now smile from cheek to cheek, initially you feel like an idiot but then it starts to feel quite good, doesn't it? This is instantaneous, that is how fast your mood and thought process can change from bad to great. You are no better or worse than the next guy but to be lifted head and shoulders above the rest or even to get the best out of yourself you've got to use the bit between your ears in a slightly different way.

I am not suggesting that if you start believing that you are the next Tiger that you will be, with your healthy one hour practice session a week when you rush straight from the office before it goes dark... Positive thinking as I explained earlier is a gradual process that requires practice, like anything else, until your brawn starts to manifest itself in your brains. There is no time like the present, your golf swing has had a make-over and your **Signature Swing** is feeling solid, so why not start to knock your brain into shape?

Take your **Signature Swing** onto the first tee with your head full of "I can't hit a cow's backside with a banjo never mind a little white golf ball" and the likelihood of you taking a divot large enough to fill a bunker starts to become reality. You would be surprised how many successful people are running around bursting with the magic ingredient who started off with the slogan "fake it until you make it" written in big letters on their fridge door. Why not convince yourself or at least tell yourself you can do it instead of "you're a worthless piece of rubbish" and then after you have hit the ball ask yourself "why me, why now?" You are only as good as you think you are, it doesn't matter what anyone else thinks, they have the same hang ups as you but nobody likes to talk about it. As soon as you start to even touch on the mental side of preparing yourself everybody runs a mile, shouting "leave me alone there's nothing wrong with me."

The great thing about trying to improve your mental game is that nobody needs to know, unless you start twitching and mumbling under your breath to yourself on the first tee. It can be a private part of your game as it is with most great players but it requires strict dedication and should be performed before every shot that you play, without compromise. Turning on the power of positive thinking and preparation at any level is a million times more productive than thinking you are crap, the choice is yours.

Visualisation is a great way to maintain your focus on the shot that you are about to play and to remain focused on your target, which, of course, is your ultimate goal. Most amateur golfers are thinking about the big tree to the left of the fairway they always hit or the water hazard that has eaten so many of their balls. If this is you then I warn you, it will be a fight in the beginning and probably a fight until the bitter end as it is with all great players. The little demons are waiting for the slightest hint of your guard being dropped and they'll knock your head sideways. Nobody is perfect and everybody is fighting with the same stuff but that's not to say that the more you stand up to the fight and go toe to toe with the demons within you won't succeed. Like anything in life you fell off your bike often enough in the beginning but you didn't let that stop you.

There are two ways to use your third eye and the power of visualisation:

 www.golfswingzone.com

- Visualise your ball going to the target exactly as you want it to
- Visualise yourself hitting the ball and watching the ball going to the target as you want it to

Your **Signature Swing** was built by your own two hands, the way your body moves and performs best. You have to try and find what works best for you. Personally I find it more challenging to visualise myself swinging and hitting the ball to the target when I'm stood on the tee rather than visualising my ball flying to the target. You are the *boss* of your **Signature Swing**, tell it what to do.

It requires practice and you have to really make an effort to drill this into your head during your pre-shot routine, without it you will never be fully in your Zone. Try not to rush; it only takes a matter of seconds anyway. None of your golfing peers will suspect anything, unless they are psychic of course. If you race through your Zone preparation and miss out the power of visualisation you'll be really missing out on something exceptional. If your mind is busy with where you want your ball to go then it has no room for anything else to get inside your head.

Your target is the only thing your mind's eye sees. Picture your best shot flying towards your target and you will be programming the most powerful computer known to man to stand up to the challenge and fight your corner.

3. Practise swings focused on your target or with your target in mind

Your brain is full with your target, nothing else will have crossed your mind and why should it? Your next step is to transfer your focus onto your target and pump this information directly into your body, programming your muscles to remember the feeling required to hit your ball to your target.

What the majority of amateurs start to throw into the pot at this stage is a waterfall of technical swing mechanics to shatter any feeling or instincts into a million pieces. Your **Signature Swing** has been built revolving around your target, so you already have a big advantage over your many wooden golfing counterparts who play golf by numbers. You are aiming for no break in concentration or rhythm, a break here and you have dropped your guard and you'd better get it up fast or it's a knock out.

Next time you watch a great player sizing up a shot you will see him feel the shot he wants to play. He will look smoothly in control, focusing on his target and prepping his body to immerse himself in the feelings and instincts that are required to take charge and excel when it matters most. This is what you will be striving for, endorsing all of the positive, target orientated energy and focusing with a feel for the distance and shape of shot that you want to play. It's no different to when you throw a ball; if you are unsure you take a few practice throws, without releasing your ball, whilst remaining fully focused on what matters most; your target. From this you can gauge the distance and direction instinctively, the way you were made to do so; you are man and far more advanced than any machine could dream of being. The technical dimension that golf offers often drowns the simple yet most effective natural instinctive side to the sport. Can you ever imagine wondering what your elbow is up to as you are throwing your ball? Not likely! So it's about time you dropped this hot potato from your game plan.

There are two methods of complementing your target mind-set with the addition of instinctive feeling for the shot you are about to play:

- Practise swings focused on your target at all times

Signature Golf Swing: Stop fighting with complicated swing mechanics!

- Practise swings visualising your target, whilst remaining focused on your ball

The aim of the game is to feel the shot that your body is about to play. I personally really like the feeling that practice swinging whilst focused on the target pumps into my body. From this I can really feel the shot that my body is about to play and I try to use the same swing feeling in my live shot. I don't try to break my swing down into bits and pieces. I allow it to flow and work as one with no pause for thought and only the target as a guide. There are other players that prefer to fill their mind with their target and imagine swinging to their target. Both methods work really well, you just have to find the one that fits your style of play. The two different methods have the same goal; to maintain that your mind's eye is fully focused on the target with the added bonus that your body gets in on the act by immersing itself in the feeling for the target.

Your body and mind are at total peace, working in harmony as one, a marriage made in heaven.

4. Stand to Attention

Align the clubface and your body correctly in relation to the target ensuring that your ball position is correct for every shot. We have already covered this earlier in **Dynamic Foundation**. It will be a formality for you now to be fully in control of how you get your body dynamically ready and aligned.

Stand to Attention and Demand Precision

a) Find a point within a metre of your ball, in line with your ball and the target line. Align your clubface to this point and address your ball correctly

b) Stand in the correct address position. Your ball is positioned in the middle of the stance

c) Place your left foot one third of the intended width of stance, parallel to your ball to target line

d) Place your right foot two thirds of the intended width of stance, parallel to your target line.

e) You will now be standing in a square position in relation to the target.

Your clubface is now perfectly aligned to your target and your feet, knees, hips and shoulders are now aligned correctly, parallel to your ball to target line.

You are now standing to attention: En Guarde!

5. Focus on your target

This is one of the key elements in the success of your **Golf Swing Zone**. If you allow your eyes to wander so will your mind. Your body will need a split second rewiring job to try, in a vain effort, to sort out the confused mess your brain has left behind, so that you can at least make contact with your ball. Your last point of focus is your target. Turn your head only and leave your body down in your dynamically ready address position, ready to fire into action. If you stand up and out of your address position like a tourist with his hand glued to his forehead, looking for his boat to come in, then yours won't. Lifting your body up and out of your set up messes with your alignment and body position which is the last thing you want to be concerned with right now.

Your last point of focus is what your body will automatically react to. If you confuse these signals your swing will be unsure of what your brain's commands actually are. As you turn your head, look at your target and wait until the picture before your eyes is clear and sharply in focus, so that your brain fully understands what your body has to react to.

6. Slowly inhale a deep breath

Now is the time to breathe. Being blue in the face is not exactly the secret ingredient to setting the stage for a free flowing, instinctively driven **Signature Swing**. Breathing fills your lungs with energy and sets off your body's natural mechanisms, pumping oxygen and blood around your body, straight into your muscles, preparing them for action. Often when we are tired or nervous we naturally try to yawn, this action is triggered for a reason. Your body is running low on fuel and needs a top up so tries to draw more energy from the blood flow that the extra oxygen creates to get things moving again. As you slowly turn your head back from your target to focus on your ball, take a smoothly controlled, big, deep breath through your nose, filling your lungs. It doesn't have to sound like an elephant sucking up a barrel of water, calm and smooth is what we are looking for here.

A fatal mistake made by the majority of amateurs is to hold their breath. You body reacts to this by tensing up and your rigid muscles don't have sufficient blood flow to support your swing the way that they should. If you relate this to weight lifting and we use a bench press as an example; as you lower the weight to your body you fill your lungs full of oxygen, preparing your body for the lift. As you push the weight away from your body you breathe out, dispelling the air from your lungs until the lift is finished. This is how your body naturally performs best, using your natural forces to the max.

7. Focus on your ball with your target in mind

Fill your head full of your target and try to remain as focused as possible by picturing your target as clear as day in your mind's eye. At first the demons within will try and tease you, in an effort to prise the positive picture out of your mind's eye, playing games with your head and attempting to force you over to the dark side of negativity.

Remain focused and keep fighting these negative influences until you regain composure and your target is the only thing in your mind. You should be aiming your focus on a small area at the back of your ball that you are about to make contact with whilst a picture of your target fills your mind's eye.

8. Slowly exhale a deep breath

A body full of air is a weak body. Try and lift a weight or perform anything that requires force and you will find that your body will naturally try and push the air out of its lungs. In martial arts you will often hear a load shout as one opponent hits the other with his fist during a punch or with his foot during a kick, delivering a powerful blow. If you watch tennis, especially the ladies, you will hear them cry out as they hit the ball, forcing the air out to squeeze every last drop of energy from their body. Your body is far stronger empty rather than full of air. To prove my point, in case you still don't believe me, go and find a partner and do the following:

- Stand tall with your arms by your side
- Fill your lungs with air
- Have your partner try to push you out of your standing position and off balance
- Repeat the same procedure but this time breathe out until your lungs are empty

Now are you convinced? A body that is empty of air is free to move and is more relaxed because the tension has been dispelled out of the body. This has a dramatic effect over your performance. Relaxed and tension free is powerful, whereas uptight and tense is weak, just how a piece of wood reacts when moist or brittle. In yoga or any simple relaxation technique for that matter, if your breathing pattern is wrong then your body will react accordingly, blocking your movements or restricting your stretch. A body that is empty of air is stronger and more receptive, resulting in a smooth, well co-ordinated, powerful golf swing.

The best method of producing a consistent release of air flow from your lungs is to breathe out through a small opening in your mouth, slowly and well controlled until your lungs are totally empty. Then and only then can you be sure that you are using your full strength.

9. React to the target. Release your swing, letting it flow freely to the target

Your brain knows full well what type of shot you want to play. Your mind's eye is fully focused on your target and your body has been pumped with all of the right feelings and instincts it needs to hit the shot that your target is waiting for.

The moment has come to react to your target and trust your built in, instinctive mechanisms that will fire into action the chain reaction of automatic physical events. Your practice swings that were focused on your target are about to come to life as your live swing emulates that of the practice swings you earlier programmed your muscles with.

Trust it, be instinctive and revolve your **Signature Swing** around your target for your Zone to take control of every shot that you play.

Top Gear

www.golfswingzone.com

Signature Golf Swing: Stop fighting with complicated swing mechanics!

With practice you will be able to switch your Zone on and off on command, your Zone is where you want to be when it matters most.

To trust your golf, place it into the hands of a PGA Professional

Time zone

Your head is loaded with information. You know how to place your body and soul in the middle of your **Golf Swing Zone** but you don't want your friends, competitors or the rules guy breathing down your neck while they wait for you. You will need to practise all nine phases of your **Golf Swing Zone** to firstly get to grips with them and secondly to build your own rhythm and timing into the procedure. It's a good idea to try this at home in your garden, working through it in your head. It won't take long until it all starts to flow and fall into place.

Each player has a different swing speed and preparation speed, nothing should dictate how quickly or slowly you place yourself into your **Golf Swing Zone**. One thing is for sure you don't want to be penalised for standing there all day getting yourself ready for your shot. If you dwell too long on your Pre-Shot Routine everything will become too stuffy and regimented. You will feel this resulting in a loss of rhythmic and instinctive behaviour towards your shots and your target. Conversely if you fly through the process at lightening speed you lose your focus which results in the same outcome as taking too long; poor golf shots through lack of focus.

The ultimate experience of guiding yourself safely into your **Golf Swing Zone** should be smoothly operated with a decisive club selection, further promoting a positive feeling. Keep it crisp and clean and let it flow. It's all a balancing act between your instincts, trust and your target. A ball park figure is anywhere between thirty and forty seconds but don't dwell on this as you know now that you can't play golf by numbers.

You are now armed with the skills to improve your golf without the often obscure guidance of running commentary breathing down your neck. The guy with the rose-tinted glasses is probably a really nice guy that you may love to bits but it's about time he put a sock in it and played his own bagpipes instead of yours.

The sweetest and most rewarding aspect of the whole **Signature Swing** building process is that you have built your swing up alone with the tools you were born with, including the fantastic piece of kit between your ears. You are a credit to yourself and a credit to me. Your improvement and enjoyment is more important to me than you could ever imagine, thank you for listening and giving me the chance to prove to you just how great you are.

You have built your own personal masterpiece that no one can ever take away from you. If the moment of reckoning comes and your **Signature Swing** hits the skids big time, calmly step back and work through the gears again until your reach your **Top Gear**. Every great player is fully aware that if he knows what went into the pie he can make it again, only next time even more exceptional than ever before.

Your Golf Swing Zone is the place you excel; go get it because you're worth it...

To trust your golf, place it into the hands of a PGA Professional

 www.golfswingzone.com

Next in the series by Lee Kopanski:

Available at www.leekopanski.com

Also by Lee Kopanski:

Available at www.leekopanski.com

www.ingramcontent.com/pod-product-compliance
Lightning Source LLC
Chambersburg PA
CBHW080737230426
43665CB00020B/2769